Ruskin, Our Enduring Bond

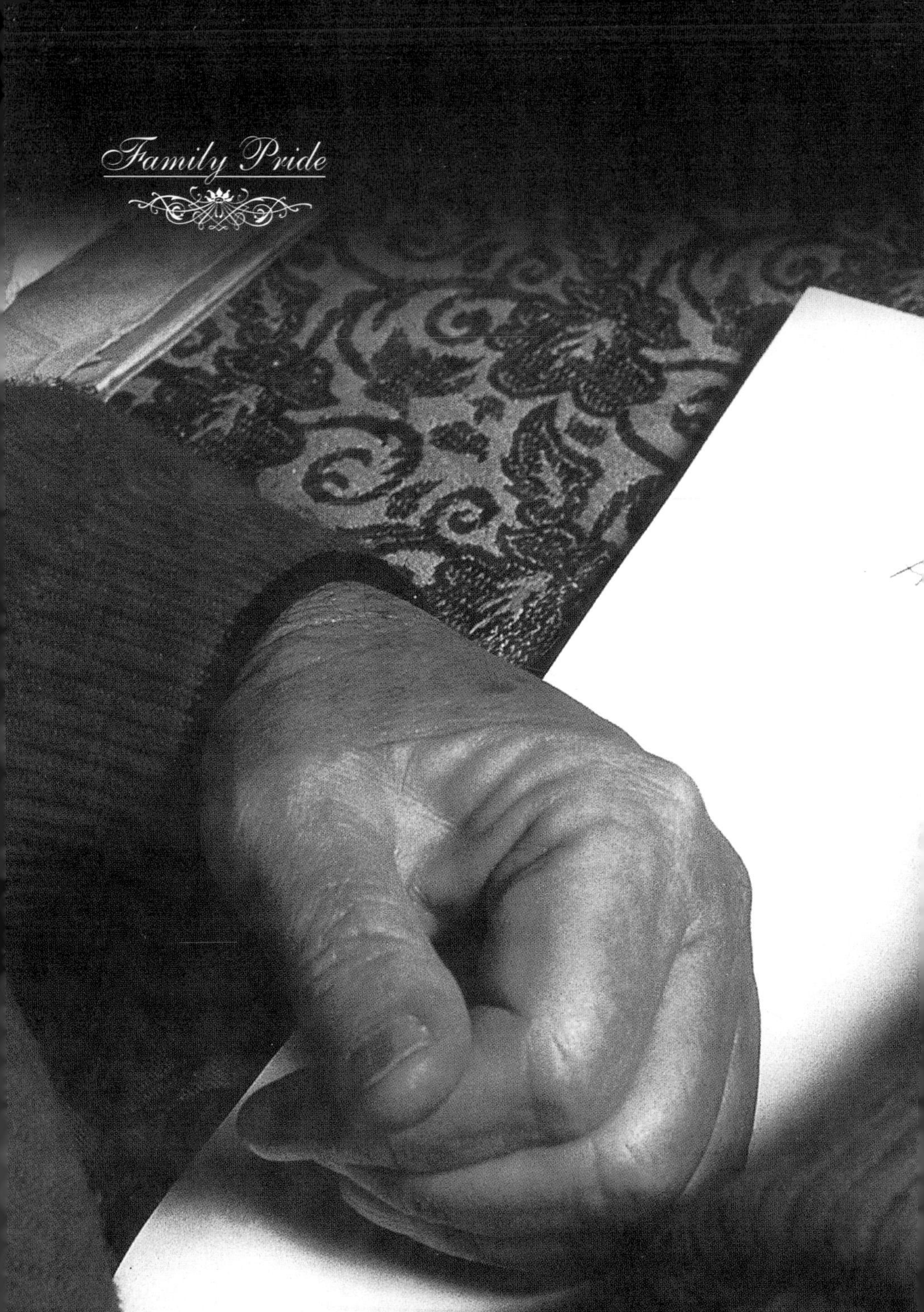
Family Pride

Ruskin, Our Enduring Bond

Ganesh Saili

Lustre Press
Roli Books

Dedication

This book is dedicated to all those at Sailgarh who've known Ruskin from the late 1960s: my wife Abha, who learnt patience from the old man of the hills; our eldest daughter Tulika, whose love for wild flowers was born from all those walks around the Landour Chakkar with him; our younger one Tania who acquired her love for books from him; my sister Punni who made sure he always had some niblets after sundown; and Meera, my youngest sister, who has since passed on, and who always called him *namkeen*. And it would be most unfair to forget Kaali, my Labrador who slobbers over him, much to his disgust. Carry on Kaali! Good luck!

Acknowledgements

I would like to thank the following people for sharing their thoughts and feelings about Ruskin: Diana Athill, William Aitken, Hugh and Colleen Gantzer, Viola Bye, Norman Van Rooy, Angela and Alan Middleton, and many others who would rather not have their names mentioned at all. A special thanks to Dipa Chaudhuri for her invaluable editorial skills.

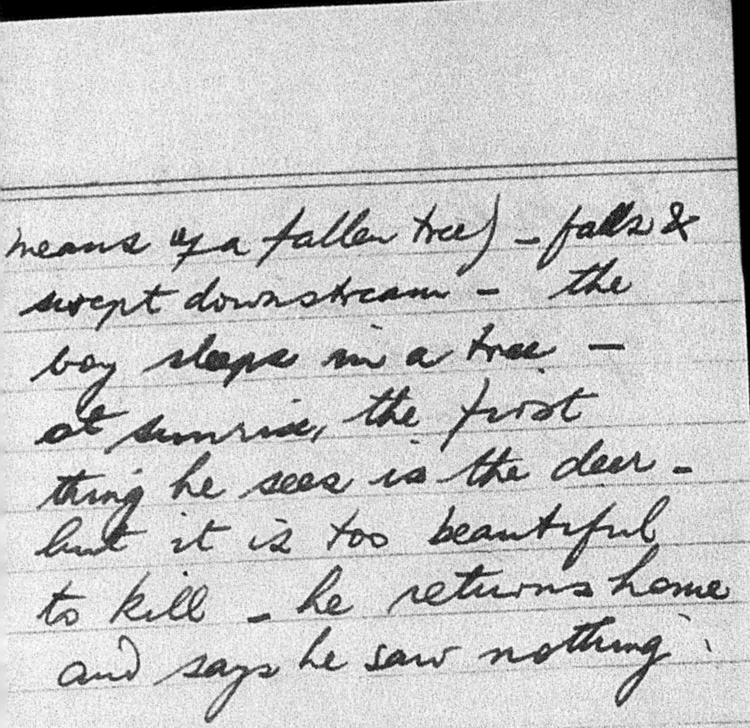

means of a fallen tree) - falls &
swept downstream - the
boy sleeps in a tree -
at sunrise, the first
thing he sees is the deer -
but it is too beautiful
to kill - he returns home
and says he saw nothing.

The outline of a story in long-hand before it is fleshed out as a typewritten manuscript.

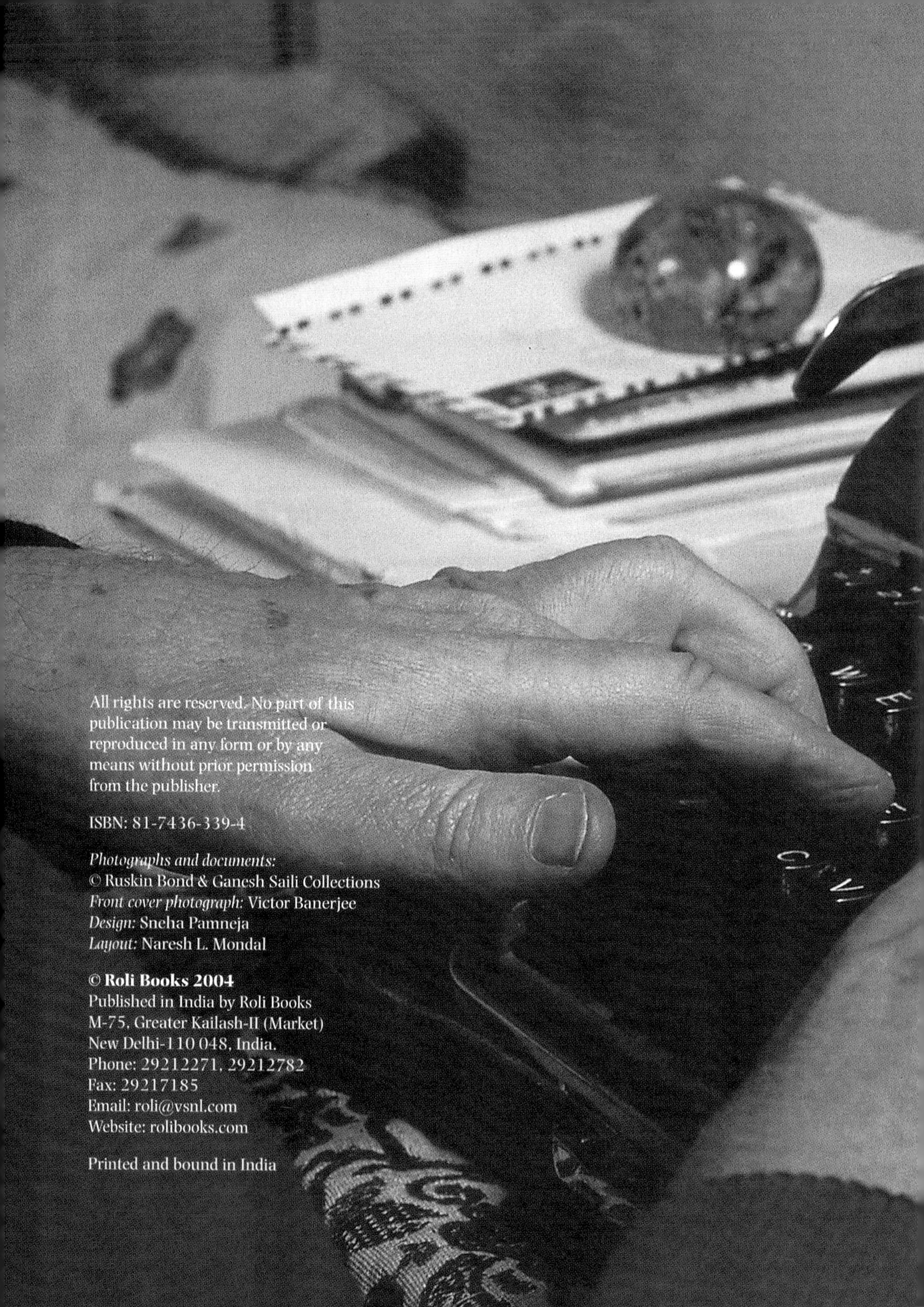

ISBN: 81-7436-339-4

Photographs and documents:
© Ruskin Bond & Ganesh Saili Collections
Front cover photograph: Victor Banerjee
Design: Sneha Pamneja
Layout: Naresh L. Mondal

Published in India by Roli Books
M-75, Greater Kailash-II (Market)
New Delhi-110 048, India.
Phone: 29212271, 29212782
Fax: 29217185
Email: roli@vsnl.com
Website: rolibooks.com

Printed and bound in India

Contents

1. Where He Comes From 13
2. Off to School 29
3. Winds of Change 61
4. Return to Dehra: Bonding with India 77
5. The Night Train to Delhi 87
6. Back to the Hills of Home 93
7. Amongst Friends 125
8. Epilogue 138
9. From Ruskin's Pen 140

7 Elsworthy Terrace
London NW3 3DR
(020) 7722 3721
July 3. 2002

Dear Professor Saili

Today is July 3, and your letter arrived this morning. It has taken three months and eleven days to make its journey. I think my American publishers must have sat on it for quite a bit before sending it on, not to me, but to my English publishers — and they must have done a bit of sitting in their turn. By now you must have written me off.

And I'm afraid that after all that I am not going to be able to help you much with material about Ruskin. It was so long ago that I'm unable to call up any specific details about our acquaintance. I can only give you a general impression of him as he struck me at the time.

I was deeply impressed by him. I had read The Room on The Roof before I met him, of course, and had been charmed by it, but not until I met him did I fully realize how young he was, how alone he was, and how he had no money at all but what he earned. And the combination of courage and common-sense which had brought him to England to find himself at once a job — a dreary one, but enough to keep a roof over his head and to feed him (though not very well) — seemed to me quite heroic. Not that Ruskin gave any sign of seeing himself as heroic. He gave the impression of thinking there was nothing special in what he was doing. How many boys (and he really was little more than a boy at the time) are so determined to write, and so calmly ready to do whatever risky or disagreeable thing may be necessary to achieve his end? The few very young writers I knew were likely to think themselves remarkable, and even tended to think the world owed them a living. There was nothing of that about Ruskin. He just got on with keeping himself independant and doing what he so deeply wanted to do.

My regret is this: although I recognized and was impressed by his fine qualities at once, I allowed myself to be a little taken in by them. Ruskin was too self-contained and too proud to make much of how hard up he was. I knew he was living on very little, but he made it look as though that very little was enough. I was very busy in those days — had a full life — but I now think I ought to have done more for him than I did: that I ought to have invited him over for a healthy meal at least once a week, instead of only now and then, as I did. Instead of just liking and admiring him in a general way, I ought to have put more into becoming a real friend to him. But of course, I was very much older than he was — he would have been hoping to find real friendship among people nearer his own age, so I don't suppose he was wanting it from me.

And anyway, he got what he wanted to get from his visit to England, and went home to take up the life he wanted to lead — the rather hard time he had while living in London did him no harm in the end. He continued to be calmly and firmly himself, as though there were nothing special about it — and that is precisely what made him then, and still makes him now, such a very special person.

I look forward to reading your biography when it's finished. I wish it the best of luck — and I'm sorry I am unable to contribute more to it.

With best wishes

Yours sincerely

Diana Athill

PS I am returning the stamp you so courteously enclosed, because the British post office will not accept it.

Ruskin's first literary mentor.

Diana Athill of Andre Deutsch, Ruskin's first publisher, recalls her association with Ruskin with pride, affection and a tinge of regret, in a letter she wrote to Ganesh Saili, Ruskin's biographer.

Where He Comes From

1

'I have no assets except the books I have written and the few that may still be lurking in the innermost recesses of my mind.'

This, dear reader, is the tale of a little boy who set out to become a writer. And did. It's not about name-dropping nor is it an eulogy of a friend who is more family, or a series of literary street-lamps arranged on a journey down a brightly-lit path to success. Of course, the journey has at times been lonely, at times solitary—there is always a fine line between loneliness and solitude—but always full of the ordinary things that shape us humans.

Success sits gently on the seventy-year-old cuddly man as he brushes away all talk of being a famous man of letters. Public recognition for his work, however, came as early as 1957, when he was awarded the John Llewellyn Rhys Memorial Prize for his first novel, *The Room on the Roof*. This was followed by years of public silence, but the writing never faltered, never slowed or stopped. The wait was worthwhile. In 1987, the Indian Council for Child Education recognized his pivotal role in the growth of children's literature in India; in 1992, the Sahitya Akademi Award honoured his contribution to English writing in India for *Our Trees Still Grow in Dehra*; and in 1999, he was awarded the Padma Shri. Of course more than all these put together are three generations of

FACING PAGE:

A man of letters.

A solitary Ruskin weaves his thoughts into a story at his writer's retreat.

schoolchildren who have become avid readers of Ruskin Bond, having grown up on a steady fare of his writings—short stories, poems, essays—now a part of school syllabi all over India. When this biography was being written, the Benares Hindu University conferred on him the honoris causa degree of Doctor of Literature in absentia.

'Why didn't you go to Benares?' I ask.

'I appreciate the gesture but it wasn't something I was looking for in life.'

Now how can one argue about that with an author whose works have been published for over fifty years by at least

Portrait of the father.

A studio portrait of Aubrey Bond taken around 1933.

RIGHT:

From Grandfather Herbert William Bond's Army Service Book.

TRUE COPY.

SOLDIER'S NAME AND DESCRIPTION.

Name: Herbert William Bond. Born 2-5-1863.

Enlisted for the Scottish rifles on 3rd November, 1883, at Bow Street Police Court, London, for 7 years with the colours and 5 years in the reserve in the County of Middlesex, at the age of 20 years, 6months.

Born in the parish of Islington in the town of London in the County of Middlesex.

Trade or calling---grocer's assistant.

Height=5ft.6". Complexion-Fresh eyes, blue. Hair brown. Religion, Church of England.
****

Marriage 4-4-1894. Jubbulpore. To Gloriana Elizabeth Enever.
****

Children.

9-2-1895. Hoshangabad Rest Camp. Herbert Henry.

29-7-1896. Shahjehanpur (Cantt). Aubrey Alexander. (1896-1944.

[illegible]-1898. Chittagong (Volunteer Hd Qrs.) Arthur Cleveland.

7-7-1902. Chatham (Fort Pitt). Gloriana Elizabeth.
****

Certified this is a true copy from your grandfather's Army Service Book.

Signed. H.H. Bond.
30/7/51.

Rifle Factory,
Ishapore.

thirty different publishers—a unique record of sorts.

'I need to write,' he tells me, adding, almost as an afterthought, 'it's like a biological need. One doesn't feel whole without putting pen to paper, again and again and again.'

And as the years roll by, the writing just keeps getting better. Age-old themes resurface constantly: remembrance of love, lament over loss that make feelings flow like a mountain stream, almost a signature of his style, then there are brief moments of silence, of pauses as he communes with nature.

He strolls into my house, as he has for thirty years and more, and sits down. I pour him a drink. Trying hard, very hard not to sound like an inquisitor from the Dark Ages, I know that like *Alice in Wonderland*, I too must start at the beginning.

'Where did your parents meet?'

'Believe it or not, but it was up here in Mussoorie!' he tells me.

It was in 1933 that Edith Clerke, Ruskin's mother, enrolled for a nursing course at the St. Mary's Cottage Hospital, and met his father, who was on vacation, having recently given up his job in a tea estate. Cupid struck, and a few months later, the two were married in Dehra. She was twenty, he thirty-six. And on 19 May 1934, Ruskin was born in the Military Hospital in Kasauli.

Ruskin's mother.

A teenaged Edith Bond née Clerke with her pet dog outside her father's house on Old Survey Road in Dehra.

Does he remember being told anything special about the time of his birth?

'Oh! Yes,' he sighs, 'I must have been born. Why else would I have a baptismal certificate with my name on it?'

Aubrey Alexander Bond, Ruskin's father, had for sometime now been working as a sort of a guardian and tutor at the highest rung in various princely states. At the time of Ruskin's birth, his father was working with the Maharaja of Alwar. In those days, if a man could afford it, he would send his wife up to a hill station for confinement. In the mid-summer of 1934, Ruskin was born at 5 a.m. on a cool May morning. To this day, he uses this as sufficient excuse to justify his distaste for getting up too early!

A few miles from Kasauli, almost next door was Sanawar, a school for the children of British soldiers, where Aubrey Bond had been educated. He still had friends there amongst the teaching staff. So that is where he went with his expectant wife. In time, Ruskin would enter the world, a chubby baby, all of nine pounds, screaming the ward down in the Military Hospital.

Kasauli was at that time famous for its Pasteur Institute that produced the anti-rabies vaccine. Gwen Stevens' husband was working at the Institute (Gwen was Edith's elder sister) and Edith stayed with them during this period. The vaccination was still in its infancy. It wouldn't keep too long. So, if a dog bit you in Calcutta, your only option was to catch a train and get to Kasauli and take your life-saving shots. If you delayed matters, you could have died of rabies. And some did get there too late. Many

Beloved Edith.

Aubrey Bond, an avid photographer and a doting husband re-shot Edith Bond's portrait amidst these decorations.

FACING PAGE:

Aubrey Bond with Emily and a friend.

Later he would marry Emily's younger sister Edith.

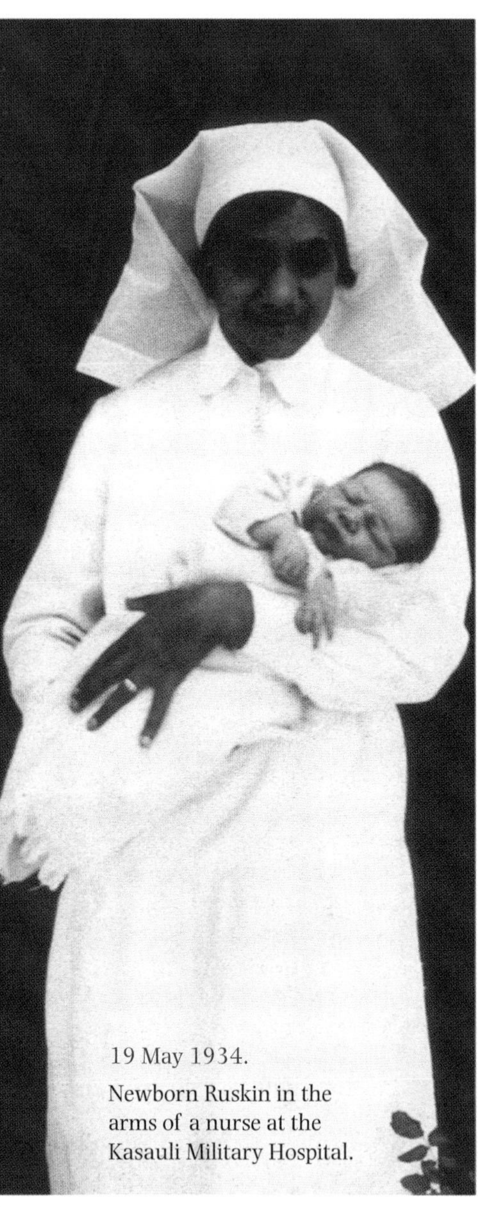
19 May 1934.

Newborn Ruskin in the arms of a nurse at the Kasauli Military Hospital.

tombstones of the Kasauli cemetery tell their sorry tales.

Ruskin was baptized in the Anglican Church which stands right opposite the local bus-stand, and was christened Owen Ruskin Bond, after John Ruskin, the famous Victorian author. Perhaps Ruskin's father hoped that one day the boy would grow up to be aesthetically inclined. When the rains set in, three months later, his parents, with three-month-old Ruskin came down from the hills to Dehra where they stayed briefly with his grandmother.

Later his father took up a job with the Jamsaheb, who had just started a little school for the children of the princely families in one of the old palaces of Jamnagar. A year-old Ruskin joined his father there.

'My first impressions of the world were of old towering palaces! Full of mystery and romance,' he says. Though he grew up with little princes and princesses, (some of those princesses, Manna, Ratna and 'Haathi' have recently, sixty years on, been in touch with him again) he found himself equally at ease with the cook, ayah and gardener. The family was never in one house or dwelling for very long. The Tennis Bungalow in Jamnagar (in the grounds of the Ram Vilas Palace) housed them for a couple of years—probably their longest stay in one place. In Jamnagar itself, they had at least three abodes—a rambling, leaking old colonial mansion called 'Cambridge House', the wing of an old palace, the Lal Bagh, which was also inhabited by bats and cobras, and the old Tennis Bungalow, a converted sports pavilion which was bright and airy.

'I think my father rather enjoyed changing houses,' he says, 'and loved rearranging rooms too, so that one month's sitting-room became the next month's bedroom and so on; furniture would also be moved around frequently, somewhat to my mother's irritation, for she preferred having things in their familiar places. She had grown up in one abode, her father's Dehra house, whereas my father had never been in one place for long.'

Ruskin's sister Ellen was born in 1935 in Dehra. In 1942, seven years later, his brother William was born in Dehra. The family lived on 6 Old Survey Road—his maternal grandfather's house since 1910. The

Days of innocence.

One of the many photographs of baby Ruskin taken by his father.

BELOW:

Old and new Jamnagar Palaces.

Ruskin spent five memorable years of his childhood in Jamnagar.

JETPUR
W.M.S.

FACING PAGE:

Mother and child.

Shortly after Ruskin was born, his father took up a job in the Kathiawar State.

children were baptized in the old St. Thomas' Church on Rajpur Road where Ruskin's maternal grandparents had been married.

Ruskin's family tree is simple. His maternal grandfather, William Dudley Clerke, was born in Dera Ismael Khan in the North-West Frontier Province, to Charles and Louisa Clerke in 1866. At that time, Charles worked there as a clerk in the Commissioner's office.

William Dudley himself worked for the railways and was one of those early pioneers who helped bring the railways to Dehra. He had two daughters from his first marriage, Enid and Beryl, and a son, Kenneth Charles. After his wife's death, he married Miss Ellen Sims in 1902 at St. Thomas' Church which is now being pulled down to make way for a high-rise. They had three daughters—Emily, Gwen, and Edith (Ruskin's

Through the father's lens.

Ruskin on the beach in Jamnagar (above), and trying his hand at tennis (below).

mother). For a couple of years Edith went to Oak Grove, a school established by the Indian Railways, at Jharipani, halfway between Mussoorie and Dehra on the old bridle path to the hills. She was to finish her schooling from La Martiniere, Lucknow.

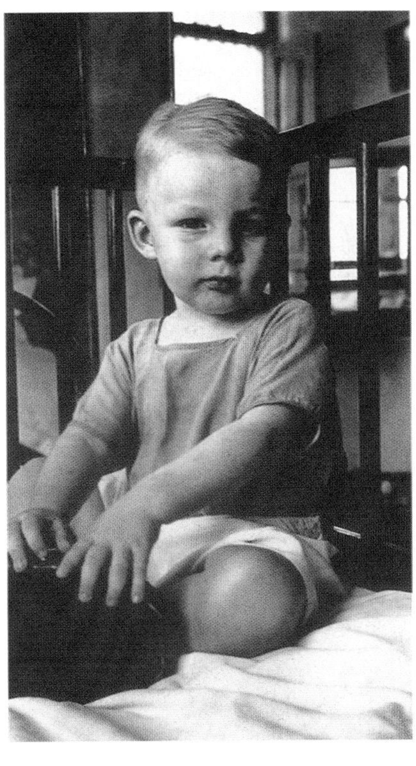

In 1935, William Dudley Clerke passed away in Dehra, where he rests in peace in the old cemetery. The family was not rich, and Ellen Clerke managed on a meagre pension, the sale of the fruit crop and by letting out half the house. She lived till about 1947.

Of all his paternal grandparents, Ruskin remembers seeing her the most. She was strong-minded, stern, and strict with her children, and lived on her own. Of Calcutta Granny, the memories are faint because Ruskin only met her once when she came to stay with his father in Delhi while he was serving in the Royal Air Force.

Ruskin is the third generation of his family in India from his father's side and the fourth from his mother's. His maternal great-grandfather, Charles Clerke, married in September 1857, a few months after the Mutiny, while his paternal grandfather left home in London at the age of seventeen and joined the Scottish Rifles in the 1880s. In 1894 he married Gloriana Elizabeth Enever, an Anglo-German who had been brought up on an indigo plantation in Motihari, Bihar.

At home.

Little Ruskin in the Tennis Bungalow at the Jamnagar Palace ground.

FACING PAGE:

At sea.

Discovering the joys of paddling with a young friend.

With young royals.

Aubrey Bond with his young wards from the Kathiawar royal family.

RIGHT:

Ruskin at the Jamnagar Palace standing next to one of the princes of Jamnagar.

'I lay no claim to descent from nobility, important families, Generals, or the like!' he says. 'My paternal grandfather was an ordinary soldier who probably had to do all the fighting. Officers, at least in those days, sat back tossing back their *burra* whisky-sodas while the foot soldiers did all the dirty work.' His mother's side comprised simple, middle-class folk.

The army in the days of the foot soldiers, in the nineteenth century, was into route marching. It was the only way to get around the country in those days. During

The Nanny's tale.

In the last row, Ruskin's nanny and Ellen's nanny stand next to each other. One of the nannies later described Ruskin, seen in the foreground here, as 'a naughty boy who always wanted to have his own way'.

the Mutiny, the troops marched from Karnal to Lucknow in the summer of 1857. If those turbulent times are mentioned to Ruskin, in his best Nelson Eddy manner, he breaks into Kipling's *Route Marching:*

Oh, there's them Indian temples to admire when you see,
There's the peacock round the corner
An' the monkey up the tree,
With its best foot first
And the road a sliding past,

King of hearts.

Ruskin turned out in regal finery for the birthday of one of the Jamnagar princes. He still likes to stand this way with his hands clasped behind him.

An 'Every bloomin' camping-ground
Exactly like the last;
While the Big Drum says
With 'is 'rowdy-dowdy-dow!'
'Kaiko Kissywarsty? Don't you hamse argy-jao!'

And so his grandfather marched, from one cantonment to another. As a result, all his children were born in army cantonments: Ruskin's father in Shahjehanpur and his uncles in Hoshangabad and Chittagong. His grandfather rose from being a private to a Sergeant Major before retiring and settling down in Calcutta where he died in his early fifties.

As an army family, the oldest boys, Herbert Henry (Uncle Bertie), Aubrey Alexander (Ruskin's father) and Arthur went to the Lawrence Royal Military School at Sanawar; Uncle Bertie went on to become a foreman at the Ishapur Rifle Factory and never married but Uncle Arthur, who was at the same factory, married twice; Gloriana outlived three of her four children and died in Calcutta at the age of eighty-six.

On finishing school at Sanawar, Ruskin's father signed up for a teacher's training course in Lovedale in the Nilgiris. Perhaps it was a vocation that suited his gentle nature. He moved from there to work as an assistant manager of a tea estate in Travancore-Cochin but returned to teaching soon after.

Ruskin didn't get to meet any of his father's relatives in those days because while the relatives lived in and around Calcutta, Ruskin stayed in Delhi, Jamnagar, Dehra and Delhi. He met mostly his mother's relatives: four sisters and a brother, who were scattered across the country.

There was an eight-year gap between William and Ruskin. The former was in school when Ruskin was growing up. Ellen was just a year and a half younger, but a forceps birth had caused irreversible brain damage. So there were not many things they could do together. William was a chubby, healthy child, who finished school in India, went off to England and later settled in Canada, never to return.

Ruskin was a quiet, sensitive child. There are people, however, who remember him as a noisy, naughty boy, who kicked and screamed and always wanted to have his way. It probably illustrates the two sides to his nature: the reflective nature, which helped him become a writer, and the zest for life that shows up occasionally in his more boisterous moods.

He speaks with glee of how once he was punished for being a little devil by being locked up in the storeroom. For the first few minutes he howled the place down, then suddenly, as if on cue, there was complete silence. Worried, his mother opened the door to discover that he had opened up a large parcel of imported chocolates, unwrapped them one by one and just to be cussed, had nibbled around the edges of every single chocolate!

Having spent the first five years of his life in Jamnagar, Ruskin learnt to read and write at home, developing rather early a taste for comics and the classics of children's literature. He remembers his father reading to him from *Alice in Wonderland, Peter Pan* and teaching him to write in a good hand. By the time he started going to school, he was around seven years old, and could already read and write.

Off to School

2

'I think I have been able to pass through life without being any man's slave or tyrant.'

In the dying years of the 1930s, the dark clouds of war had begun to gather over Europe. In 1939, when World War II broke out, Ruskin's father, in his early forties, joined the Royal Air Force as a pilot officer in the cipher section at the Air Headquarters in New Delhi. Ruskin's mother moved to Dehra to live with Grandmother Clerke and Ruskin was sent to a boarding school—Convent of Jesus and Mary at Hampton Court, in Mussoorie.

Of his first day in school, Ruskin says, 'Oh! It had nothing to do with reading or writing. It was terrible. I kicked and screamed. My mother had come to drop me off as my father was away with the RAF. I didn't like the idea at all. I think I even kicked the Reverend Mother on her shins! Perhaps one of the reasons I was never very popular with her.'

True! He never really settled down at Hampton Court, and hated the place each day of the year and a half that he was there. It wasn't a cruel place but it lacked character of any kind; it really was a staging post or a waiting room for boys and girls going on to bigger schools in the hill station. You took nothing away and you left nothing behind. In those days, the nuns were strict and

FACING PAGE:

The war years.

Ruskin near Salan village in Rajpur getting ready to leave his school in Mussoorie and move on to Delhi for a year before going to his new school in Simla.

FACING PAGE ABOVE:

Granny Clerke with mother.

Edith Clerke, still a schoolgirl with her mother. Ruskin was born to her three years later, when she was eighteen.

FACING PAGE BELOW:

Mother's day out.

Ruskin's mother leaning against Aunt Enid during a picnic in the foothills near Dehra, in 1942.

unsympathetic; the food was awful (stringy meat boiled with pumpkins); the boys were for the most part dull and unfriendly, and the girls too subdued. Ruskin had started taking piano lessons, probably at his father's behest. The nun who was teaching him would, in exasperation rap him on the knuckles whenever he hit the wrong note! Not surprisingly, he soon abandoned the piano.

However, Ruskin still remembers a boy he liked and with whom he used to share his desk. They would often plan to run away together. So they would save their tuck—bits of bread, rusks, and other nibbles. Everything would eventually become hard and mouldy. They never did get the opportunity to run away. But that did not stop them from planning to escape from a prisoner-of-war camp, as it were.

Yet there was no escape. He had to put up with Hampton Court for over a year because his father was being moved, first from Calcutta to Delhi, then from Delhi to Karachi. And his mother was in the midst of an affair with his future stepfather, whom Ruskin had seen occasionally in her company, and whose presence Ruskin deeply resented.

One day, in the middle of the term, much to Ruskin's bewilderment, his mother turned up unexpectedly and withdrew him from school. He was to find himself not at his grandmother's place in Dehra but at the railway station to catch the night train to Delhi, without an escort or a chaperone.

'I was off, aboard the train, hurtling into the dark night on my own,' he remembers, adding, ' and it was very soon after that I learnt of my parents' separation. I was to be in the custody of my father, Ellen would stay with Calcutta Granny and William would be with my mother.'

Looking back sixty years later, Viola Bye, (née Melville) an old family friend, now settled in New Zealand recalls: ' I think Ruskin was rather a lonely, private person and maybe that is why he found his outlet in writing and maybe his life was sad too. But I think he is also a very caring and dedicated human being... His grandparents were of my grandparents' generation and I met them through my parents' visits in Dehra where I was born and lived all my childhood, except when I was in school in Simla. Mrs. Sims, Ruskin's great-grandmother was a tiny, very active, white-haired lady with bright blue eyes, always up at 6 a.m. to take in and boil the milk before her daughter Mrs. Clerke was up! Ruskin's grandmother was a much larger lady than her own mother, and was married to Mr. Clerke, who retired in 1925. He had a brother, Major Clerke who wore a full beard and moustache and lived with his wife, a tall white-haired lady, who always smelt of lavender and kept miniatures in a glass case. Their house was just off Rajpur Road leading down to the Rispana, before Dilaram Bazaar. Ruskin's grandparents had two daughters, Emily, who married Dr. Heppolette and eventually was my gynaecologist. They had

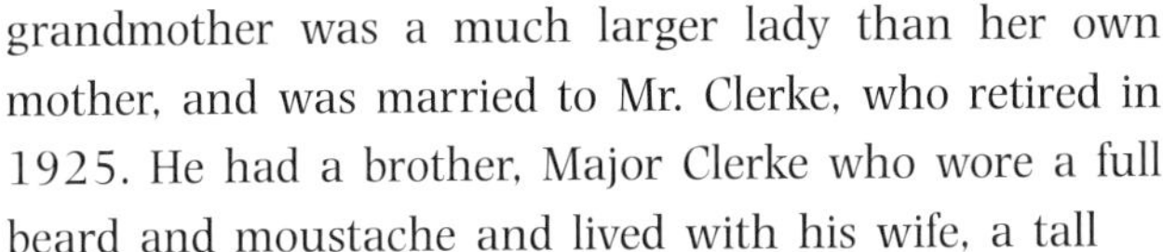

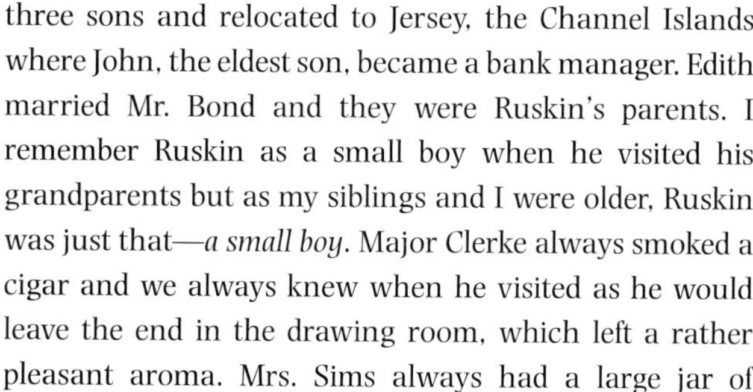

three sons and relocated to Jersey, the Channel Islands where John, the eldest son, became a bank manager. Edith married Mr. Bond and they were Ruskin's parents. I remember Ruskin as a small boy when he visited his grandparents but as my siblings and I were older, Ruskin was just that—*a small boy*. Major Clerke always smoked a cigar and we always knew when he visited as he would leave the end in the drawing room, which left a rather pleasant aroma. Mrs. Sims always had a large jar of strong mints that she brought out when we visited and we each got one!'

In Delhi with father.

During the war years, Ruskin stayed with his father in temporary hutments (below) and often wore khakis and his father's RAF cap (facing page).

Gradually, Ruskin learnt that his mother was involved with a Punjabi businessman, Mr. H.L., a dealer in second-hand cars, who owned an auto repair shop and had left his wife because of this liaison.

On Ruskin's arrival at the Delhi railway station, he remembers meeting his father all dressed up in his khakis and blue RAF cap. It was only during the meal that Ruskin surmised that his parents had separated. Looking back today, he feels that those brief years with his father were probably the happiest years of his childhood.

From 1942 to 1943, Ruskin lived with his father in the temporary wartime hutments, possibly without official clearance. Despite his father's failing health, he gave Ruskin his time, companionship, and his complete attention. So, though Ruskin saw no schooling during this period, he never complained about it. He could go to the movies, to Davicos, Wengers, read books, listen to records, examine his father's stamp and postcard collection while he waited for his father to return from his duty and take him wherever he wanted to go.

During their stay in Delhi, Ruskin remembers changing houses five times—Aubrey Bond and Ruskin first lived in a tent on a bald plain outside Delhi, before moving into a hutment near Humayun's Tomb; from here they graduated to a couple of rooms on Atul Grove Road, then to Hailey Road before finally settling in at Scindia House, facing Connaught Place. Often, Ruskin would watch his father rustle up breakfast for him. Aubrey Bond encouraged Ruskin to keep a journal. To begin with, just lists of singers, movies and records, later it was to give Ruskin the discipline of writing regularly, by recording all he saw and observed.

Of the years spent in Simla, Ruskin has only pleasant memories, And Simla will always hold a special place in his affections. It was in Simla that he went to school, and it was here that his father and he spent their happiest times together. They stayed on Elysium Hill, took long walks to Kasumpti and around Jakko Hill, sipped milk-shakes at Davicos, watched plays at the Gaiety Theatre (happily still in existence), fed the monkeys at the temple on Jakko Hill, and picnicked in Chhota Simla. The short

A world of words.

Ruskin inherited his love for literature from his father. This was one of the many rhymes that Aubrey Bond had taught his little son.

summer break when his father, on leave from the Air Force, came up to see him were full of these activities. He told Ruskin stories of phantom-rickshaws and enchanted forests and planted in him the seeds of his writing career.

Ruskin was only ten when his father died. But Aubrey Bond had already passed on to his son his love for the hills. And even after Ruskin had finished school and grown to manhood, he was to return to the hills again and again—to Simla and Mussoorie, Himachal and Garhwal—because, as he put it: 'Once the mountains are in one's blood, there is no escape.'

Not that he really wanted to go to Simla, to Bishop Cotton School, then called the 'Eton of the East.' He tried every argument he could think of to change his father's mind. He pleaded that he would learn much more at home. That he would be lonely. But his father was being posted to Karachi. The only other option was for Ruskin to go stay with his mother. The prospect didn't please him. So, he settled down in Bishop Cotton without any fuss.

Compared to the old Mussoorie convent, Bishop Cotton was a luxury. Due to wartime shortage, food was rationed but the school continued to serve up great omelettes made from egg powder. The benevolent Ram Advani, then the school bursar, remembers Ruskin joining the school mid-term in Class I, fifty years ago!

In 1943, nine-year-old Ruskin was placed in Ibbetson House (the other three being Curzon, Lefroy and Rivaz). The year went by quite fast and at the end of the school term, he was back with his father in Delhi for the three-month winter break. The movie halls, bookshops and restaurants were just a stone's throw from Scindia House, and he was happy and contented. They went for long walks to the Purana Qila and Humayun's Tomb, surrounded by the wilderness of trees. Those days there were very few cars in Delhi and the only big hotels were the Maidens and the Swiss in Old Delhi.

From Karachi with love.

This was the last picture taken of Ruskin's father (left) during his posting at Karachi. Ruskin did not see him ever again.

During the last few years in school, Ruskin became rebellious and even submitted an examination paper with the observation: 'Exams are rubbish!'

The worst thing he remembers doing around this time is smashing the windowpanes of the school library door. At times he was good, at times temperamental. At fifteen he was a good athlete, the football team's goalkeeper and a fine hockey player. He remembers Mr.

Jones, who helped him learn the breaststroke to overcome his fear of water. At studies, he was poor in Maths. He was very good in English, History, Geography, and the arts but at the sciences, he was less promising. While in the first few years, Ruskin did well, in the senior classes, he couldn't concentrate on the science subjects.

One of the boys with him at Bishop Cotton was Geoffrey Davis, the great-grandson of Pahari Wilson of Hursil. Geoffrey's mother lived in Ashley Hall, Dehra. 'We used to call him "Chinky" Davis, because of his almond-shaped eyes,' he reminisces. On finishing school, Geoffrey joined the Air Force and was later killed in a flying accident. His late grandfather, Charlie Wilson, had earned a certain distinction by going to jail for fraud. It was said that he came out of jail a rich man, having bankrupted all his friend and associates.

Charlie Wilson's father had been the famous Pahari Wilson who had made a fortune as the Raja of Tehri's contractor in the 1860s, being the first man to float timber down the Bhagirathi River. This made him the first large-scale exploiter of the forest reserves of this region. He married a village girl, Gulabi, and settled down to the good life in Hursil and Mussoorie. Hunting elephants, horses, carriages, fine houses in several beautiful spots... these were only some of Wilson's many assets.

The Bishop Cotton School football team crest.

Ruskin was the school football team's goalkeeper.

Perhaps his most spectacular achievement was the building of a 350-feet suspension bridge over the Jad Ganga at Bhaironghati. It connected two rocky promontories over the turbulent Bhagirathi. We learn in Andrew Wilson's *Abode of Snow* that because of its dizzy height and ultra-vision span, this bridge proved a source of terror to travellers and only a daring few ventured across the rippling contraption. To reassure people, Wilson assembled a host of Brahmins who kindled a sacred fire and chanted hymns. On this auspicious occasion five score goats were slaughtered in sacrifice. But even then, the bridge was not for the faint-hearted. So Wilson mounted his half-Arab Grey and galloped it too and fro across the bridge. Something of the legend finds its way into Ruskin's story, *Wilson's Bridge.*

***

On Ruskin's return to school in the spring of 1944, his father was transferred to Calcutta, where Aubrey Bond lived with his mother and Ellen at 14 Park Lane. Since Calcutta was too far away from Simla, it was no longer possible to make those fleeting visits to Simla during the school breaks, but Aubrey Bond made up for it by writing to Ruskin regularly. These letters gave Ruskin a sort of window to his father's world—news of Calcutta, Granny and Ellen, the stamp collection and the records. Occasionally he would advise Ruskin on how to improve his writing style. He looked forward to Ruskin's Calcutta visit in the winter of 1944. But his own health was failing; he had weakened due to malaria and passed away a few weeks later from hepatitis.

The only 'survivors' from those days of childhood are a few postcards from his father while he was at Hampton Court. His father's last letter to him was at Bishop Cotton in Simla. He had kept a number of his earlier letters. But after his father's death, the headmaster, Priestley found him poring over them and took them away saying he could collect them at the end of the term. When Ruskin finally went and asked Priestley for the letters, he looked confused and couldn't remember having kept them. For a ten-year old, this was a cruel blow. Today he dismisses Priestley as a poor absent-minded headmaster.

It did not occur to anyone to arrange for Ruskin to attend his father's funeral, which made it all the more difficult for him to deal with this irreparable loss (see pp. 58-59). Years later, the feeling has not left him as he says: 'As there was no evidence of my father's death, it was, for me, not a death but a vanishing, and to this day, I subconsciously expect him to turn up (as he indeed often did, when I most needed him) and deliver me from bad situations.'

For the next fifty years, he saw his father as a protective guardian as he lived out his life by what his father had taught him. It was only in the winter of 2001, at the age of sixty-seven, that he was able to bring himself to believe that his father was gone when he visited the Bhowanipore Cemetery in Calcutta. Flight Lieutenant Aubrey Bond was laid to rest by his own mother, Gloriana. Ruskin remains grateful to Maya Banerjee, the wife of actor Victor Banerjee for all her help and assistance in locating the grave.

Postcard from father.

Most of the letters Ruskin's father sent him were lost by the headmaster Priestley at Bishop Cotton. But Ruskin still has a few postcards his father sent to him while he was at Hampton Court.

With his father gone, Ruskin resented having to perforce spend his winter vacations with his mother and his stepfather in Dehra. The first homecoming after his father's death was an agonizing experience for Ruskin. No one had come to receive him at the railway station and he had no idea what his mother's new address was

7145 Town Hall, Simla.

Bryanston Simla. 11-10-1941

VALENTINE'S "LAWSON WOOD" POSTCARDS. COPYRIGHT.
VALENTINE & SONS, LTD., DUNDEE AND LONDON.

3360

My, darling Ruskin,
Thank you for your nice letter. I am glad you had a good time at the Fancy Fair. You were very lucky to win a top. I am leaving Simla in 14 days time. Did you hear from mummy. She is in Dehra Dun. "Beauty" is also with her. Mr Jenkins sent "Beauty" by train last week. Ellen must be very glad to [illegible] once again. Write again [illegible] God bless you. Have a good week darling, Your loving Daddy. xxxx

POST CARD
FOR CORRESPONDENCE
FOR ADDRESS ONLY

Master Ruskin Bond.
Convent of Jesus & Mary.
Hampton Court.
Mussoorie.
U.P.

INDIA POSTAGE

(see p. 85). So he took a tonga to the only place he knew—Granny Clerke's house on Old Survey Road. Later, he was to find out that his mother had got the dates mixed up and had instead gone off with Mr. H.L. for a shikar, having left William and his two half-brothers in the care of servants.

'He never said a harsh word to me ever!' Ruskin says of his stepfather. But he did feel neglected and lost.

On being asked which parent he took after, he says, 'Who knows who gave me what? Perhaps my sensuous nature from my mother and the cerebral part from my

FOLLOWING PAGES:

Calcutta 1944.

Despite his failing health, Ruskin's father took care to write letters that would encourage and nurture a passion for all things aesthetically pleasing, in his son.

F/Lt. A A Bond 108485. (RAF)
C/o 231 Group,
Raffpost
Calcutta. 20/8/44.

My dear Ruskin,

Thank you very much for your letter received a few days ago. I was pleased to hear that you were quite well and learning hard. We are all quite OK. here, but I am still not strong enough to go to work after the recent attack of malaria I had. I was in hospitall for a long time and that is the reason why you did not get a letter from me for several weeks.

I have now to wear glasses for reading, but I do not use them for ordinary wear but only when I read or do book work. Ellen does not wear glasses at all now.

Do you need any new warm clothes? Your warm suits must be getting too small. I am glad to hear the rains are practically over in the hills where you are. It will be nice to have sunny days in September when your holidays are on. Do the holidays begin from the 9th of Sept? What will you do? Is there to be a Scouts Camp at Taradevi? Or will you catch butterflies on sunny days on the School Cricket Ground?

I am glad to hear you have lots of friends. Next year you will be in the top class of the Prep: School. You only have 3½ months more for the Xmas holidays to come round, when you will be glad to come home I am sure, to do more Stamp work and Library Study. The New Market is full of book shops here. Ellen loves the market.

I wanted to write before about your writing Ruskin, but forgot. Sometimes I get letters from you written in very small handwriting as if you wanted to squeeze a lot of news into one sheet of letter paper. It is not good for you or for your eyes, to get into the habit of writing too small. I know your handwriting is good & that you came 1st in class for handwriting, but try and form a larger style of writing and do not worry if you can't get all your news into one sheet of paper - but stick to big letters.

We have had a very wet month just passed. It is still cloudy - at night we have to use fans, but during the cold weather it is nice - not too cold like Delhi and not too warm either - but just moderate.

Granny is quite well. She and Ellen send you their fond love. The last time I heard a week ago, that William & M at Dehra were well also.

We have been without a Cook for the past few days. I hope we find a good one before long. There are not many. I wish I could get our Delhi Cook, the old man now famous for his "Black Puddings" which Ellen hasn't seen since we arrived in Calcutta 4 months ago.

I have still got all the Records & Gramaphone and most of the best books, but as they are all getting old & some not suited to you, which are only for children under 8 yrs old — I will give some to William & Ellen, and you can buy some new ones when you come home for Xmas. I am re-arranging all the stamps that became loose & topsy-turvy after people came & went through the Collections to buy stamps. A good many got sold, the rest got mixed up a bit and it is now taking up all my time putting the balance of the Collection in order. But as I am at home all day, unable to go to work as yet, I have lots of time to finish the work of re-arranging the Collection.

Ellen loves drawing. I give her paper and a pencil and let her draw for herself without any help, to get her used to holding paper & pencil. She has got expert at using her pencil now, and draws some wonderful animals like camels, elephants dragons with many heads - cobras - rain clouds shedding buckets of water - tigers with long grass around them - horses with manes and wolves & foxes with bushy hair. Sometimes you cant see much of the animals because there is too much grass covering them or too much hair on the foxes & wolves and too much mane on the horses necks - or too much rain from the clouds. All this decoration is made up by a sort of heavy scribbling of lines, but through it all one can see some very good shapes of animals elephants & ostriches & other things. I will send you some.

Well Ruskin I hope this finds you well with fond love from us all. Write again soon. Ever Your loving daddy XXXXX

Flowers for father.

Nearly fifty-seven years after his father passed away, Ruskin finally located his grave in the Bhowanipore War Cemetery, Calcutta with the help of Maya Banerjee, actor Victor Banerjee's wife.

father. Or maybe a bit of both. And a lot from my grandparents—including Granny's double-chin!'

As Diana Athill, his literary guide and mentor at Andre Deutsch notes in a letter written to Ruskin fifty years after *The Room on the Roof* was first published: 'Of course, your father had a lot to do with it. It made me almost weep to know that he was not there to see his beloved son going his own way so bravely and making such a success of it, but Ruskin seems a wonderfully clear example of something I have come to believe since the death of my own mother, which is that a child doesn't—indeed cannot—*really* ever lose a truly loving and beloved parent because so much of that parent remains actually *in* the child: the genes of course, which amount to an actual physical presence, and an incalculable amount of shaping and patterning acquired during their shared life. Although Ruskin and his father were able to share only a short part of life, that part was composed of by far the most formative years... Yes! He made Ruskin a writer, and that is Ruskin's centre.'

Memories of those early years of childhood are not at all dreamlike and idyllic. Ruskin watched his parents quarrel, and later, when things took a turn for the worse, his mother would leave for destinations unknown (unknown only to him).

He says: 'In my writing, I often appear to be taking my father's side. Well! He stood by me, an eight year old. Naturally I resented my mother's liaison with another man.'

Today he has learnt to accept human nature and says expansively: 'She was only eighteen years old, outgoing, fun-loving when they met in Mussoorie. My father was fifteen years her senior. Years later she told me that he was very jealous, and kept her away from other men. Of course anyone would have been jealous. She was young, pretty, and vivacious—heads turned wherever she went. But all this discord left me helpless and insecure, a feeling that has never left me.'

Mr. H.L. and Ruskin's mother's frenzied partying and hectic lifestyle got them nowhere socially in a small place like Dehra at that time. The snootier Anglo-Indians cut Ruskin's mother off for having married Mr. H.L., an Indian. With money running out, their relationship went through difficult times. So, when Mr. H.L.'s second business venture, an auto repair garage, failed, he and Ruskin's mother parted company and she started working as the manager of Green's Hotel (which has since vanished and become a cinema hall), while Mr. H.L. moved back, albeit temporarily, with his first wife, who ran a small a provision store.

By 1948, Calcutta Granny was over eighty, and too old to look after Ellen, a girl with many medical problems. True, the RAF did send an allowance for most of Ellen's maintenance, but looking after her put further constraints on Ruskin's mother.

'They were irresponsible with their money,' says Ruskin about his mother's second marriage. 'Mr. H.L. and my mother set out to enjoy their lives instead of paying their bills in time.'

His stepfather's auto repair garage was a financial disaster. If a car was left behind for repairs, he would be driving around town in it for the next few weeks. If this was ever mentioned to him, he would reassure people by saying that it was taken out for a 'test-drive, for the good of the car!'

In 1945, the business failed. Ruskin's mother and Mr. H.L. were evicted from a house in Dalanwala and took refuge in Grandmother Clerke's house. Mr. H.L. even invested money in an ambitious project for a film called *Frontier Mail*, which never saw the light of day. While Ruskin was in England, they lived behind the Orient Cinema in the old Gresham Hotel in Dehra; finally they had to leave Dehra because of mounting financial pressures. Mr. H.L. ended up as Sales Manager at Sikand Motors, thanks to his old friend Mr. Sikand in New Delhi.

All this while, a teenaged Ruskin felt insecure. He would lie awake endless nights wondering how the family

FACING PAGE:

Playing fields.

Ruskin on a visit to Sanawar in 1947 to play football for his school team.

would manage if something fatal were to happen to his mother and stepfather. There would be nobody to fall back on if his mother and Mr. H.L. were to get killed in a car accident or in the jungle. Mr. H.L. did have a serious accident and was in hospital with burns and broken bones, but fortunately lived to tell the tale.

Ruskin turned to books to cope with his increasing loneliness. He devoured whatever he could lay his hands on—from Grandmother's house to the Ideal Book Depot, which also ran a lending library. To get away from the domestic quagmire, he would go to the movies or visit his grandmother and her physically challenged tenant, Miss Kellner. He got on well with older people. They could tell him stories of their lives and about growing up in different parts of India. Apparently, when Miss Kellner was a baby, an uncle used to toss her up in the air. One day he fumbled as she came down. She fell and hurt her spine, and was crippled for the rest of her life. A small mercy was that her parents had left her enough money to carry on. She paid Ruskin's grandmother her rent on time and had four, liveried rickshaw-pullers, who lived in the outhouse and were called out for the rare occasions on which she would go out for card parties. Ruskin could never really play cards, so she taught him simple card games that he would try out with her, or listen to her stories. He enjoyed the generous goodies she would serve him.

Another friend of those troubled times was Dukhi, an elderly gardener who had worked for his grandmother for many years. He liked having long conversations with Ruskin who would tell him stories without interrupting the flow of his gardening activities.

Mr. H.L. made feeble attempts to be nice to Ruskin, taking him along for hunting trips to the nearby Motichur and Dhaulkhand forests. But these fumbling forays into the wild left Ruskin cold. After a few such excursions, he preferred staying back in the Dak Bungalow, while the others tramped off in search of game. In the Dak Bungalow he discovered a treasure trove of books! The shelves were lined with books by P.G. Wodehouse, Dickens, the Bröntes, and the ghost stories of M.R. James. Hungrily he devoured them all. When he looks back on those times, he remembers that his stepfather was such a poor shot, that one could hardly hold him to task for the absence of wildlife today, but he did do his best to eliminate every creature that strayed within sight.

Back in Bishop Cotton, Ruskin was put in charge of the library which he turned into his private retreat where he frenetically read everything he could lay his hands on. He worked his way through most of the library from 1947 to 1950. The range was vast: adventure and mystery, the novels of Hugh Walpole, R.M. Ballantyne, Charles Dickens, the complete plays of Bernard Shaw and J.M. Barrie. The short stories of A.E. Coppard, H.E. Bates and William Saroyan wove their spell on the young Bond, a magic that suited his own gentle nature. It was easier to reach out to fleeting sensations than look for profundities when there were none in his own life.

Of course Ruskin always kept a diary, a habit that led him into trouble more than once: the first time was at Bishop Cotton, for, at some point in his journal, he went into raptures over the comely shape and generous proportions of his housemaster's wife. His class master discovered the diary in his desk, read parts of it and sent him off to the housemaster's study where Bond received a dressing down. In retrospect, though, he remembers that the housemaster kept the diary and believes that perhaps his wife read it too, and was secretly amused and possibly flattered by the account of her physical attributes! Anyway she went out of her way to be nice to Ruskin, and to this day, he remembers that she even held his hot, sweaty hand for a while when school closed and it was time to bid goodbye. The housemaster though, was not as warm.

'My first attempt to write a novel or a memoir was at school in Simla when I was thirteen. It was called *Nine Months*, but had nothing to do with pregnancy; it referred merely to the length of the school term—beginning-March to end-November—and it entailed my friendships, escapades, ambitions, and views on life in general, and also described the foibles of some of our masters. It filled two exercise books and lay in my desk for a couple of months. These too were discovered by a master, and torn to shreds and thrown into the wastepaper basket.' Ruskin feels the master did him a favour. He is the first to admit that this was no great work of literature

The habit of keeping a diary did get him into trouble again many years later in his aunt's house in Jersey (in the Channel Islands) where he went to stay, at the age of seventeen. Unable to contain his curiosity, his uncle had

Homeward bound.

At the end of the term in 1950, Ruskin relaxes in the winter sun before going home for holidays.

dipped into the diary and read some critical remarks about his relatives' diehard colonial attitudes. There was an awful row in the house after that, and Ruskin packed his suitcase and took the boat to Southampton from where he journeyed up to London. That was when he wrote his first novel, *The Room on the Roof.*

During the eight years of school in Simla, Ruskin was popular with the other students, especially the Indians. To his peers, he was a hero because of a mischievous streak in him that made him play pranks, answer back and upset masters. He excelled in sports especially football (he was the school team's goalkeeper from 1948 to 1950). 'I've always been a goalkeeper, guarding my goal, my way of life.'

The school records show that his skill in writing won him the Hailey Literature Prize in 1949 and 1950; the Shakespeare Award in 1949; the Anderson Essay Prize in 1948, 1949 and 1950. Ruskin was the only student in the history of the school to have won this prize for three consecutive years!

A marathon run.

Ruskin receiving a trophy in 1951 at Bishop Cotton on Sports Day.

Besides these laurels, he also has the distinction of having his name inducted in the school's Hall of Fame. He shrugs it off and says: 'Of all the prizes I got, the acting prize pleased me the most. In the play *Borrowed Plumes*, an old fashioned farce, I played the part of a drunk to perfection, and that too on plain, cold tea in a whisky bottle. My experience of my stepfather's booze parties had stood me in good stead after all!'

He was in the school choir, something people on the hillside, who have heard him sing, find hard to believe, but he insists: 'Oh! Yes I was! But they told me not to sing because I had a terrible singing voice. Apparently I looked quite cherubic in a cassock and surplice, and was told by our choir mistress to open my mouth along with the others, but on no account to allow any sound to issue forth!'

No easy task that, considering that Ruskin was an ardent fan of Nelson Eddy, a singer in the classical mould. But many have ever since specifically forbidden him to sing in a car, for, the moment he begins to sing, the vehicle is guaranteed to have a flat tyre!

The roller coaster at school continued and 1950, Ruskin's last year at Bishop Cotton, proved to be a watershed of sorts for him. He found himself on the wrong side of the school administration, rebelling against authority, in a state of permanent revolt against tradition, convention, and examinations. His bête noire was the new headmaster, who had just taken over a year ago. Mr. Fisher and his wife were the wrong people at the wrong place at the wrong time. They would play favourites and heap invectives on their young charges. So it was hardly surprising when, two years later, in 1952, the Fishers

ANDERSON ESSAY OPEN COMPETITION

Winning Essay,

" THESE HAVE I LOVED "

"Give me the sea, give me the sky,
Give me the sun that shone;
Give me the eyes, give me the soul,
Give me the lad that is gone."

Here lies a shell. I picked it up many years ago when I was running along the sandy beach which sloped down to the sea. It struck me because of its vivid colour,—a rich Prussian blue—and I have kept it with me since. It brings back memories. Laying it to my ear I can hear the wind and the waves as they buffet the rocks; and picture the swallows circling the lighthouse, and hear the seagulls crying in the night. Floating on this wave of memory comes the beloved sound of my mother's voice and the pattering of my little sister's feet as she comes skipping down the garden path.

... changing tides, they came and went like ... out to sea again. Many were sincere. ... seasons of fortune: they were the ... the day, the fair wind of my setting-out ... steadfastness had in it the miraculous ... power not merely to comfort and ... essential quality of love. I chose ... give my reasons; but it was at ... reasons which reason does not

... rough the long passage of time. ... pondering over this dream of ... back like vague undefined

The Playing Fields of Simla

One morning after chapel, the headmaster announced that the Muslim boys—those who had their homes in what was now Pakistan—would have to be evacuated, sent to their homes across the border with an armed convoy...

...It was soon time for Omar to leave—he along with some fifty other boys from Lahore, Pindi and Peshawar. The rest of us—Hindus, Christians, Parsis—helped them load their luggage into the waiting trucks. A couple of boys broke down and wept. So did our departing school captain, a Pathan who had been known for his stoic and unemotional demeanour. Omar waved cheerfully to me and I waved back. We had vowed to meet again some day...

...Towards the end of the school year, just as we were all getting ready to leave for the school holidays, I received a letter from Omar. He told me something about his new school and how he missed my company and our games and our tunnel to freedom. I replied and gave him my home address, but I did not hear from him again. The land, though divided, was still a big one, and we were very small.

Some seventeen or eighteen years later I did get news of Omar, but in an entirely different context. India and Pakistan were at war and in a bombing raid over Ambala, not far from Simla, a Pakistani plane was shot down. Its crew died in the crash. One of them, I learnt later, was Omar.

Did he, I wonder, get a glimpse of the playing fields we knew so well as boys?

Perhaps memories of his school days flooded back as he flew over the foothills. Perhaps he remembered the tunnel through which we were able to make our little escape to freedom.

But there are no tunnels in the sky...

FACING PAGE:

Bishop Cotton School, Simla.

Ruskin was the only student in school to have won the Anderson Essay open competition for three consecutive years. *The Playing Fields of Simla*, was inspired by his days in Bishop Cotton, and a classmate.

FACING PAGE:

Of exemplary character and abilities.

Despite Ruskin's rebellious nature in his last years in Bishop Cotton, his school-leaving character certificate was rather laudatory.

were asked to leave for a host of other reasons as well. As a sixteen year old, the final year in school left a lasting impression on Ruskin—a strong dislike for the elitist attitude the public school system reinforced in those who studied there, more so as almost all those who studied there came from affluent families.

In the winter of 1951, having finished Senior Cambridge, Ruskin returned to Dehra where his stepfather and mother gave him a small barsati-room, above the old Gresham Hotel. He was still resentful of his mother's marriage to Mr. H.L. and did not want to stay with the family. All he wanted at this point was to break free and get some measure of privacy so that he could get on with his life and write. 'There was never any desire to go to college or get more degrees,' he says. 'Henceforth I was content furthering my education in second-hand bookshops!'

Domestic discord became an integral part of his life, till, one day, after a quarrel with his mother, he walked out of home, and spent the next few days on railway platforms and park benches. With time, he realized that he couldn't spend the rest of his days as a homeless vagrant, and returned home to announce that he would stay on only until he found a job. No words were exchanged, and he was given his own room on the roof of the old building where they lived. It wasn't much of a room, but had a window from which he could look out at the trees—and beyond the trees, at the Himalayas.

GOVERNMENT OF INDIA.
MINISTRY OF DEFENCE.

TO WHOM IT MAY CONCERN.

Mr. OWEN RUSKIN BOND, son of Fl/Lt.A.A.Bond, has been personally known to me for a very long time. He was a student of the Bishop Cotton School for a period of 8 years and was successful in the Senior Cambridge Examination. His work and bearing at School were such that he was made House Captain for two years consecutively. He did well both in the classroom and the field of sports. He also revealed literary talent; several of his short stories have been published in various magazines in India.

I have great pleasure in testifying to his exemplary character and abilities.

M S Himatsinhji

Major-General
(M.S.Himatsinhji)
11 Oct 51.

The Funeral

'God has need of your father ... .' With those words a well-meaning missionary had tried to console him.

And had God, in the same way, laid claim to the thousands of men, women and children who had been put to rest here in these neat and serried rows? What could he have wanted them for? Of what use are we to God when we are dead, wondered the boy.

The cemetery gate stood open but the boy leant against the old stone wall and stared down at the mourners as they shuffled about with the unease of a batsman about to face a very fast bowler. Only this bowler was invisible and would come up stealthily and from behind.

Padre Lal's voice droned on through the funeral service and then the coffin was lowered—down, deep down—the boy was surprised at how far down it seemed to go! Was that other, better world down in the depth of the earth? How could anyone, even a Samson, push his way back to the surface again? Superman did it in comics but his father was a gentle soul who wouldn't fight too hard against the earth and the grass and the roots of tiny trees. Or perhaps he'd grow into a tree and escape that way! 'If ever I'm put away like this,' thought the boy, 'I'll get into the root of a plant and then I'll become a flower and then maybe a bird will come and carry my seed away... . I'll get out somehow!'

A few more words from the Padre and then some of those present threw handfuls of earth over the coffin before moving away.

Slowly, in twos and threes, the mourners departed. The mist swallowed them up. They did not see the boy behind the wall. They were getting hungry.

He stood there until they had all gone. Then he noticed that the gardeners or caretakers were filling in the grave. He did not know whether to go forward or not. He was a little afraid. And it was too late now. The grave was almost covered.

He turned and walked away from the cemetery. The road stretched ahead of him, empty, swathed in mist. He was alone. What had his father said to him once? 'The strongest man in the world is he who stands alone.'

Well, he was alone, but at the moment he did not feel very strong.

For a moment he thought his father was beside him, that they were together on one of their long walks. Instinctively he put out his hand, expecting his father's warm, comforting touch. But there was nothing there, nothing, no one ...

He clenched his fists and pushed them deep down into his pockets. He lowered his head so that no one would see his tears. There were people in the mist but he did not want to go near them for they had put his father away.

'He'll find a way out,' the boy said fiercely to himself. 'He'll get out somehow!'

Chronicle of a death.

In *The Funeral* Ruskin wrote about the event that would change his life forever—the loss of Aubrey Bond, his father.

Winds of Change

3

'We all know that life is finite, that human civilization, for what it's worth, is self-limiting.'

The Raj was coming to an end. Grandmother Clerke passed away on the eve of Indian Independence, at the age of seventy-six; Aunt Emily, his mother's eldest sister, inherited her house. A year later she married Dr. John Heppolette, sold that house of memories, and like all the other aunts who were leaving India, left for the greener pastures of Jersey in the Channel Islands. Soon, only Ruskin's mother remained in India.

By 1951, Ruskin had begun to write seriously in order to be published. 'There were few outlets,' he says, adding, 'so, if one my pieces was rejected by *The Illustrated Weekly of India* or *The Sunday Statesman*, I would send it off to *My Magazine of India* published from Madras, for which I would get five rupees. There was a lot you could do with five rupees in those days! But one day I received a money order for two rupees and eight annas from them. I shot off a protest letter to the editor asking why?' "Simple!" He wrote back, "We've deducted one year's subscription to the magazine!" '

Ruskin's first story was published in *The Illustrated Weekly of India* in 1951. It was called *My Calling*—a light humourous piece on one of his masters. *The Weekly*

FACING PAGE:

Emulating Eddy.

Ruskin with his Nelson Eddy puff photographed in 1950 in Dehra. A few months later, he left for England.

FACING PAGE:

Ship to England.

The P & O Liner *Strathnaver* on which Ruskin travelled to England in 1951. After sailing from Bombay, it called at Aden and Marseilles, before docking at Tilbury, London.

published the next one as well. It was called *The Untouchable*—a straightforward piece, neither childish nor juvenile. No excesses, no flourishes and very spare. It fetched him fifty rupees.

For some time now, Ruskin had been toying with the idea of going off to England to fulfil his dream of becoming a writer. He felt that in England he would be closer to the literary world. As luck would have it, an old insurance policy that his grandmother had taken out for him matured around that time. He now had enough money to pay for his journey to Jersey in the Channel Islands, where Aunt Emily lived. She had written to Ruskin's mother saying that he could stay with her until he found his bearings.

In the autumn of 1951, at the age of seventeen, Ruskin took a train out of Dehra, bidding farewell to the comforts of home, the warmth of friends, to head towards a land unknown. It was not easy giving up things familiar. His last entry around this time in the Dehra journal says: 'To love and to be loved is the greatest happiness.... Men and women leave the age of childhood behind, and are so busy with their buyings and sellings, their ambitions and their hopes, their loves and their hates, that they forget they once lived in a land where dreams were natural. I will not forget my childhood, I shall not surrender it.'

On a cold winter's day in November 1951, Ruskin sailed aboard the P & O Liner *Strathnaver* from Bombay's Ballard Pier for London and then to Jersey in the Channel Islands. He describes his arrival in England in his first poem titled *Lost* which he sent from Jersey to C.R. Mandy, the editor of *The Weekly*.

I boarded the big ship bound for the West,
The clean white liner.
In the noon-day heat
Coolies thronged the sun-drenched pier.
Yet I saw only
The village I had left,
And a boat at rest
On the river's shallow water
In the shade of the flowering
Long red-fingered poinsettia.
I saw not the big waves
But the ripple of running
Water in the reeds.

We came to London, lost in November mist:
In an ash-grey dawn at Tilbury dock
I longed for the warmth of a kiss
Of sunlight.

In the busy streets
Were cavalcades of people
Hurrying in a heat of hope.
But I saw only

The wheat-field, the tea-slope...
A cow at rest.
And longed for the soft, shoeless tread
Of a village boy...

With just a couple of pounds left in his pocket, he knocked on Aunt Emily's door.

In St. Helier he did the rounds of the solicitors' offices, hopeful of becoming a clerical assistant, but that was not to be. Everyone found him too young. One firm wanted him to join as a tea-boy. Finally, he started off on a pittance in Le Riche's grocery store. Ruskin did not

like the store. For one, the hours were too long—he would have to be there before sunrise and perforce, return home after dark, way past sunset. And then, the other clerks had nothing to commend them. Only on half-days like Saturdays or holidays could he escape those humdrum surroundings to wander around the island soaking in the atmosphere, getting a 'feel' of the place, or watching the high tide rush in or the low tide ebb.

Back at Aunt Emily's home, in the retreat of his little attic, which he had more or less to himself, he slowly started putting down the sights, sounds and smells of Dehra in the journal he had kept during the last year there. All those friends of adolescence came back to life again, resurrected from memory to become characters in the yet untitled novel which would one day be called *The Room on the Roof*. Remembering those early days, he says, 'I was only seventeen. But out of my loneliness I produced a novel, raw, naive and imperfect, but brimming with life and joy and truth, my own truth, for to be true to oneself is to be true to others... In my forties or fifties, I began to write in a nostalgic way. And perhaps *The Room on the Roof* is the only exception as I was in an alien land, far away from the familiar atmosphere of India.'

In 1952, as he sat in a theatre in St. Helier, watching Jean Renoir's film *The River* based on Rumer Godden's novel by the same title, his stories *Untouchable* and *Maharani*, began to appear in *The Illustrated Weekly of India*. Around this time, a kindly soul, Mr. Bromley, impressed by the dedication of the young would-be writer, loaned Ruskin money to get a typewriter. By the end of the year, he had already submitted his manuscript to three publishers in London. One of them, Andre Deutsch, liked his work but suggested he come to London to discuss a few changes. On his solitary wanderings along the beach, he resolved to get away from Jersey and go to London and become a 'real' writer, no matter what.

With just twelve pounds in his pocket, he left Jersey for London. For once, he was completely on his own—it

FACING PAGE:

Jersey seafront, the Channel Islands.

Ruskin arrived at Aunt Emily's house in Jersey with a couple of pounds in his pocket.

was freedom at last! He found a job, a regular nine-to-five, for six pounds a week, at a company that dealt in photographic equipment. And at one point in time, briefly, he did find himself living in a garret, like one of those starving poets.

London, for a stranger, was a lonely place. Being alone in London was akin to being the loneliest person in the world. The loneliness of London is the loneliness of those thousands—millions perhaps—who are forced to live alone in poky little bed-sitting-rooms, in gloomy suburban houses, with plaster peeling off the walls, a common lavatory to serve the needs of about a dozen residents. Ruskin's own room smelt of gas (the gas-pipe leaked occasionally), and was bare of any colour or design. The bed was full of bugs, the cracked mirror distorted his image, and the previous occupants had used the curtains as towels. He had this room to look forward to every evening, when he finished work in the office in Soho. It was a depressing home, and he could not afford a better one, not on six pounds a week, his salary at the age of eighteen. His only consolation was that there were thousands of others living just like him—native Englishmen and visiting students from the Commonwealth, many of whom had lost interest in their studies and taken up jobs instead.

Evenings were the loneliest part of his life. His days were spent in a busy office, his nights with the book he was writing; but between five and eight in the evening there was a waiting period, a marking time, when to sit alone in a cold room, in front of a miserable little gas-fire that didn't even look warm, eating the inevitable beans on toast, was intolerable. At such times Ruskin would go out into the

FACING PAGE:

Down and out in London.

Life in London was a solitary and dismal fare for Ruskin who held out in the hope of being published there some day.

streets and walk for miles, sometimes blindly, dreaming of an Indian summer. Sometimes he walked with his eyes open, trying to see as much as he could—through the East End, Soho, along the river. But the people he saw wore masks, the imperturbable, pale masks of Englishmen, which so infuriatingly hid their more human side.

He would watch the ships pass under the bridges, going to all those corners of the world where he would rather have been. He tried once to get a job on a ship, just as a deck hand, but failed. Even as a deck hand, one had to have some sort of qualification. He was chained to London, and didn't have the money to return to his friends and family in India. But he persevered and saved a pound every week for the day when he could set sail for India.

His craving for love and companionship drove him to a prostitute—one of those painted mechanical women, from whom all humanity had been drained out, and who would slip out from behind the murky lanes behind Piccadilly, to whisper 'Come along darling' in a voice as unemotional as a fishmonger's—and his experience with her only made him lonelier.

After almost a year of a dull and dreary existence though, a little colour did come into his life. He met some West Indian, colourful, flamboyant youngsters, who held a party in his room one night. George from Trinidad played the piano with his huge black hands; Eric, slim and coffee-coloured, stamped his feet rhythmically on the floorboards; and Rose, a ripe and pretty girl of sixteen, put her arms around Ruskin and taught him the calypso.

The following morning he was evicted by the landlord and had to find another room.

Ruskin had grown used to living on his own in small rooms furnished with other people's spare beds, tables and chairs. He had grown used to the print of Constable's *Blue Boy* on the wall, even though he had never cared for the look of that boy. But those London bed-sitters had been different. Whether in Hampstead, Belsize Park, Swiss Cottage or Tooting, they had been uniformly lonely. One seldom encountered other lodgers, except when they came to complain that the radio was too loud; and the landlady was seen only when the rent fell due. If you wanted company, you went out into the night. If you wanted a meal, you walked down the street to the nearest restaurant or snack bar. If you wanted to kill time, you sat in a cinema hall. If you wanted a bath you went round to the nearest public bathing rooms where, for two shillings and six pence you were given a small cake of soap, a clean towel, and a tub of piping hot water. The tub reminded him of his childhood days in Jamnagar, where he would be soaped and scrubbed by a fond ayah; but there was no fond ayah in London. And rooms with attached baths were rare—and expensive.

Of course, Ruskin had quite a variety of landladies and landlords, as he moved a great deal from one bed-sitting-room to another. The first one was a very cold attic, in which the gas leaked. Since he was afraid of gassing himself, he would throw open the window and the fog would roll in. There was just one bathroom for all the tenants in this building and a big notice board which said 'Please don't throw your tea leaves in here.'

A few years after the war had ended, two friends from Germany, Kasper and Andrious came visiting. They had been in school with Ruskin in Simla. The nationality of the visitors had upset his Jewish landlady, and she didn't want them around. Anyway they stayed for a night, as he tried to explain to her that they had grown up in India, not in Germany. She, however, was glad to see them leave.

Later he had another landlady who would make him really nice breakfast and give him a hot water bottle. She even came to visit him in the hospital when he was admitted for an eye ailment. Another landlord was peevish, but would give him kippers for breakfast, but he didn't stay long because the room gave on to a cemetery—not the most cheerful of prospects. Then he went to another boarding house where girls were not supposed to visit him.

That was when Ruskin was friendly with Vu-Phuong, a Vietnamese girl. They took walks together over Primrose Hill and she would tell him his fortune with tea leaves. In fact she even predicted that one day he would be famous. He was quite devoted to her and accompanied her to a village near Newbury where she was to spend summer picking strawberries with about a hundred other girls. Unfortunately, he was not permitted to join the girls in the strawberry picking.

He wanted to marry her and even proposed to her, but she left to visit her parents in Vietnam, never to return. To this day, Ruskin treasures the memory of that early, unrequited love.

Later, he moved to another place where the proprietors didn't mind anyone visiting him. His experiences were varied indeed with one constant—in the 1950s London was prejudiced against foreigners and coloured people.

When Ruskin had the money, he went to the theatre—*Porgy and Bess*, *Teahouse of the August Moon*,

FACING PAGE:

Fifty years later.

Extract from a letter written by Diana Athill of Andre Deutsch to Ruskin fifty years after she had edited *The Room on the Roof*.

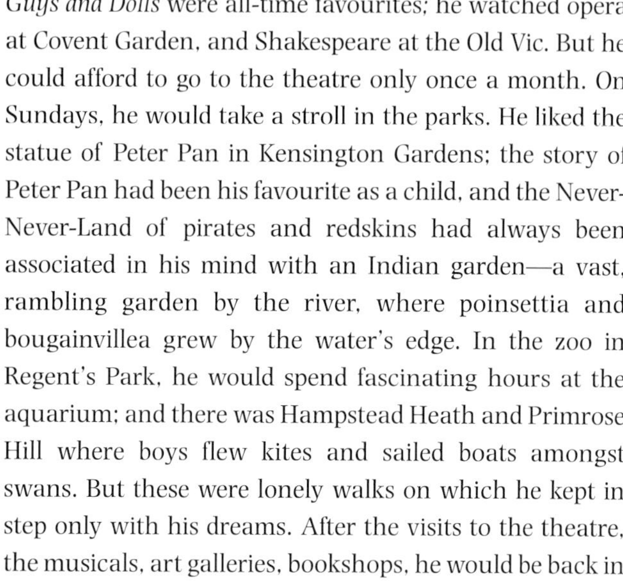

Guys and Dolls were all-time favourites; he watched opera at Covent Garden, and Shakespeare at the Old Vic. But he could afford to go to the theatre only once a month. On Sundays, he would take a stroll in the parks. He liked the statue of Peter Pan in Kensington Gardens; the story of Peter Pan had been his favourite as a child, and the Never-Never-Land of pirates and redskins had always been associated in his mind with an Indian garden—a vast, rambling garden by the river, where poinsettia and bougainvillea grew by the water's edge. In the zoo in Regent's Park, he would spend fascinating hours at the aquarium; and there was Hampstead Heath and Primrose Hill where boys flew kites and sailed boats amongst swans. But these were lonely walks on which he kept in step only with his dreams. After the visits to the theatre, the musicals, art galleries, bookshops, he would be back in his room to continue working on his novel.

The novel was constantly undergoing changes. One publisher would ask him to flesh it out, only to have the second one ask him to prune it a bit. So, what was initially a journal, evolved into a first-person narrative before ending up as a third-person account! Two things about it, though, never changed—the warmth of adolescent friends and the title, *The Room on the Roof.*

At Andre Deutsch, the publishing house, he was to meet the tall, auburn-haired Diana Athill, who became his mentor in those early days of struggle. Ten years his senior, she took him under her wing, fed him and kept a sisterly eye on him, and filled up the literary

BELOW:

The first novel.

The first cover of Ruskin's first novel, *The Room on the Roof,* published by Andre Deutsch.

I can't tell you how delighted I am to learn That I once could be described as "angular". I see from The 1996 & 97 photos That there is now rather more of "Author" then there used to be — but not anything like as much more as There is of me! My memory for names has become terrible, so I can no longer recall the name of The (alas) rather tiresome young man who once brought me a novel because you had given him my name, and whose novel turned out to be an orgy of egocentricity so That I turned it down, & who Thereafter became rather a thorn in my flesh by writing me endless black-mailing letters saying That his Mother had put all her faith in me and would now go into a terminal decline unless I changed my mind about his novel .... Well, just The other day, many many years after he last crossed my path (by coming into The office and falling into a cataleptic fit so That we had to call an ambulance & get him to hospital — and later That day, when I called to enquire, The hospital said he'd recovered & left, & I had no idea of his address, so That was That) — all those years after That, a letter arrived addressed in his still-unmistakably loopy writing, & what it said was That he'd been walking along Finchley Road when suddenly he had seen "a very stout lady with a cheerful expression" — and had realised it was me. So he was writing to say how horrid I'd been not to go to The hospital with him in The ambulance!.... I wonder how he has managed to survive in London for so long.

I am enjoying being retired a lot — much more Than poor old Andre, who is my senior by three weeks but who seems sadly much elder, partly because he never had anything in his life but his firm — he has an obsessional nature and it fastened on that to The exclusion of almost everything else — and partly because he's less lucky Than I seem to be in his vacuum in his life. Fifty years later, in a letter to researcher Meena Khorana, she recalls, 'He was such a brave little figure... . I do remember thinking that never never would I have had the courage to launch myself across the world like that, or the steadiness to then plod on in the dreary job he found, so sensibly and uncomplainingly. For such a young person he had an amazing amount of dignity, of an utterly unpretentious kind.'

And slowly, she began to like the way the book looked—from a first- person journal to a work of fiction in the third person. As she remembers: 'What made me want to publish him was simply the book itself...[I] was struck by how totally free his writing was of the kind of fault often apparent in the writing of young and unsophisticated people driven by a longing to be a writer. So often they feel it necessary to strive for a sophisticated effect, instead of trusting their own voices. But this boy had the innate good judgement to write about what he really knew, in his own voice. And the result, of course, was a freshness and authenticity which was charming as well as genuinely interesting.'

Meanwhile, Ruskin had begun to miss a few cherished things: the affection, the camaraderie, the simple pleasures of friends in Dehra; the sounds, the smells, the sights of India that he had left behind. Though he had been brought up with a love for the English language and its literature, and despite his ancestors being British, England was not for him. He did not belong there. He belonged, very firmly, to 'the peepul trees and the mango groves; to the sleepy little towns all over India; to hot sunshine, muddy canals, the pungent scent of marigolds; the hills of home; spicy odours, wet earth after summer rain, neem pods bursting; laughing brown faces; and the intimacy of human contact.'

He had been away from his roots for over three years. And though he knew that there was no job or fortune awaiting him on his return, the yearning for home was too strong. What would he do once he got there? He did not know. All he had for certain was a lot of faith, best expressed in his motto, 'Never despair. But if you do, work on in despair.' To top it all, he had all the optimism of the young.

In August of 1953, he dashed off a letter to Andre Deutsch demanding that his manuscript be returned: 'I fully appreciate the delay, and was not over-anxious when June turned to July, and July to August, and still there was no contract and still no news.

'However, August 1953, is a long way off from December 1952, when I first came to you, and though I am aware and appreciative of the many ways in which I have benefited from my perseverance with your firm, I now feel that I have been "on the rack" long enough and that I deserve a final decision.

'I would like to stress my appreciation of the fact that you are busy people, and that whilst I have only one book to worry about, you have scores; and I also appreciate the fact that I am very young and can therefore be made to wait. Indeed, I am only too glad to wait, provided I know there is something to wait for...

'I have not wanted to write this letter, because I have not wanted to hurry you, because to hurry you might have been to spoil my chances. But I must risk offending you by asking that you please give me your final decision by the end of the month.

FACING PAGE:

Back to Dehra.

While his first novel was being published in London, Ruskin returned to Dehra in 1955. This photograph was taken at Ramneek Studio near Odeon Cinema. The studio and the cinema have since disappeared.

'If this letter has already convinced you of my utter unsuitability for the role of one of your authors, I would appreciate the return of my MS of *The Room on the Roof*. I do not ask for any favours, I want no friendship. I only want business.

'If you have incurred any expenses on my behalf, such as the payment of fees to readers, please send me a bill for the same. '

Back in the mail, came a fifty pound advance against royalties (that's what one got in those days) from his would-be publishers. With this money, a small fee from a story he had sold to the BBC and a bit of his savings from his job, he bought a ticket on the Polish ship, the S.S. *Batory* and set sail for home—India.

It had taken him two years to save up enough money to leave England. Even when he was on the boat-train, headed for Southampton, he feared that something would prevent him from leaving. The urge to leave had been so great, the wait had been so long, that he couldn't be sure of his good fortune. It was only when his ship had sailed into the Channel that he heaved a sigh of relief, smiled again, thumbed his nose at England, and allowed himself to feel a little affection for the miserable old city of London.

As the ship docked at Port Said, he and another Indian student were invited by a guide to view a sexual orgy. The guide led them down an alley, through one door and out of another. After a couple of beers in a bar, their guide handed them over to another fellow, who took them past the souks into another bar and after another round of beers, he too vanished.

'We almost missed the boat, and never saw the legendary sexual odyssey!' says Ruskin a bit ruefully.

Return to Dehra: Bonding with India

4

'Happiness is an elusive state of mind, not to be gained by clumsy pursuit.'

'Dehra then was not a place for young men setting out to make a career. But I was lucky. Bibiji, Mr. H.L.'s first wife, took me under her wing and I soon had my own room on the roof! She ran a provision store downstairs and lived in the room behind it.'

Ruskin returned to India in the spring of 1955, with his first book accepted for publication, brimming with confidence that he would make it as a successful writer in Dehra. After arriving in Bombay, he caught the train to Delhi where his stepfather received him. Later, he learnt that Mr. H.L.'s business had folded up, and that he, along with Ruskin's mother, his sister Ellen, his brother William, and his two half-brothers, was planning to go to Delhi.

Rumour had it that Bibiji *actually* chased people around with an axe. 'Yes, it's true, but the axe was reserved for my mother and stepfather, I think! She would fly into fits of rage and chase her son around the block if she thought he was spending too much money. Overweight and suffering from hernia, she was grateful to me for bringing back a hernia pack for her from London. Of course, abdominal supports weren't common in those days.

FACING PAGE:

Call of the hills.

Even though Dehra was not the finest of places for Ruskin to make a career, especially in writing, the call of the hills was difficult to resist.

'I had left India with two suitcases and returned with two. Actually, the young Arab from whom I had bought one of those suitcases had assured me that it was made of special camel-skin. It must have been a very old camel, because it fell apart even before I had reached Dehra.

'It was later that I heard I had got the John Llewellyn Rhys Memorial Prize. Had I been in England for a few more months I could have actually attended the function. But I was in India when the novel was serialized in *The Weekly*. There weren't many papers that reviewed books then, but it was reviewed in Britain quite extensively. And there were many encouraging reviews in *The New Statesman* and *The Guardian*.'

But the advance from Andre Deutsch had melted away, and the book had yet to be published. Ruskin would have to write and sell some short stories and articles—and soon, if he was to survive in the India of 1955.

'But money talks!' he says. 'Mine was usually saying goodbye.'

Indeed, most of his money had gone in paying for his passage back to India. By the time he arrived in Dehra, he had about Rs. 800 to show for his years abroad. It didn't help to learn that his stepfather had gone bankrupt, and that his stepfather and his mother were planning to start a new life in Delhi, free of the encumbrance of a non-functional auto repair garage and unmanageable income tax arrears. If they were hoping that Ruskin would return from England with his fortune made, they must have been sorely disappointed.

Within a couple of months of Ruskin's return, his mother and stepfather, with his school-going brother and half-brothers, his handicapped sister and his mother's dogs (about six of them) in tow, left for Delhi. He, however, did not accompany them, for he had not returned to India to live in Delhi. And while he had nothing against dogs, he did not fancy sharing a small flat with a number of yapping poms, pekes and dachshunds.

Ruskin wanted to be near old friends; he wanted new friends. He wanted the familiar lanes of Dehra; its trees and gardens. He wanted the proximity of the hills and rivers. And, above all, he wanted the freedom of being his very own person.

Bibiji lived in the back of her shop and seldom came up to his room. She hadn't been able to pay the electricity bill for a couple of years, so the supply had been cut off and Ruskin was without electricity. Not that he particularly cared. He lit candles for a few days. But when he realized that he could neither read nor write by candlelight without getting a headache, he bought a kerosene lantern and sat it upon his desk.

His 'desk' was really a large dining table on which were spread out notebooks, paper and his typewriter. A couple of smooth rounded stones from the Rispana riverbed served as paperweights. There was a framed photograph of his father—forty years on, it is still on his desk—and one of Vu-Phuong, the Vietnamese girl from whom he hoped to hear some day. As months went by and he received no news from her, or of her, the photo moved from its frame into his albums and remained there marking the memory of a distant dream.

Of course there had been other girls too. It would have been nice to see Raj again, the pretty Punjabi girl with whom Ruskin had played badminton the year before

At Rishikesh.

Ruskin fording the Ganga at Rishikesh around 1957-58.

he left for England. A fine, athletic girl, she used to beat him 15-0, 15-1 (the last point in his favour being an act of mercy on her part). He, of course, would put up with these walkovers just to be with her.

'Oh! The things we do for love!' he reminisces. But Raj's father, like Ruskin's stepfather, had lost his money in ill-conceived business ventures, and left Dehra with his family.

So, at long last, Ruskin was where he had yearned to be, but without a job, and with no prospects of getting one either, just propelled by a raw determination, a wild courage to be a writer, and to write. This he did with great gusto.

'I bombarded every magazine in the country with short stories, essays, articles and they all paid, even the *Sainik Samachar* paid Rs. 25! I was an impractical sort of fellow and all my friends felt that perhaps it would be best if I could stick to the only thing I could do well—put pen to paper!

'In the mornings, I would do my thousand words. Then I would wander around with my friends, from one café to another or eat at wayside *dhabas* or on a good day go to upmarket restaurants. Afterwards, it was back to the solitude of my room.'

He had found the one thing he cherished—freedom—and that he was not going to give up.

This was a period of frenetic creativity. Ruskin wrote some of his best short stories in collections like *The Night Train at Deoli* and *Time Stops at Shamli* during this period. These include haunting tales of youthful romance, of unrequited love, and of parting. What remains is the treasured memory of what might have been.

He had just turned twenty-one that year.

'Oh yes!' he recalls, 'I remember that morning forty-nine years ago, when I saw my first novel in print!' (He had yet not received a copy of the one being published in England). He was up a little earlier than usual, well before sunrise, well before Bibiji called out for him to come down for his tea and *parantha*.

It was going to be a special day and he wanted to tell the world about it. But when one is twenty-one the world isn't really listening to you. He bathed at the tap, put on a crumpled but clean shirt, trousers that needed cleaning, and shoes that needed polishing. He had never cared much about appearances. But he did have a nice leather belt with studs that he tightened around his waist. He was a slim boy, just a little undernourished. On the streets, the milkmen on their bicycles were making their rounds. Stray dogs and cows were sniffing at dustbins. A truck loaded with bananas was slowly making its way towards the *mandi*. In the distance he could hear the whistle of an approaching train.

A dip in the Ganga.

Having cycled from Dehra to Rishikesh in 1957-58, Ruskin decided to cool off in the Ganga

A couple of small teashops had just opened, and Ruskin stopped at one of them for a cup of tea. As it was a special day, he decided to treat himself to an omelette. The shopkeeper placed a record on his new electric record player, and the strains of a popular film song pervaded the neighbourhood. The song was about a girl's red *dupatta* being blown away by a gust of wind and then retrieved by a handsome but unemployed youth. Ruskin finished his omelette and set off down the road to the bazaar.

It was a little too early for most of the shops to be open, but the National News Agency would be open and that was where he was heading. And there it was, with piles of fresh newspapers piled up at the entrance. *The Leader* from Allahabad, *The Pioneer* from Lucknow, *The Tribune* from Ambala, and the bigger national dailies. But where was the latest issue of *The Illustrated Weekly of India*? Was it late this week? He did not always get up at six in the morning to pick up *The Weekly*, but this week's issue was a special one. It was to start serializing his novel. It was *his* issue, his special bow to the readers of India and the whole wide beautiful wonderful world.

Mr. Gupta popped his head out of the half-open shop door and smiled at him. 'What brings you here so early this morning?'

'Has *The Weekly* arrived?'

'Come in. It's here. I can't leave it on the pavement.'

Ruskin produced a rupee. 'Give me two copies.'

'Something special in it? Did you win the first prize in the crossword competition?'

Ruskin's hands were not exactly trembling as he opened the magazine, but his heart was in his mouth as

Uncle Mulk.

Mulk Raj Anand sent this card to Ruskin in 1994, expressing his appreciation of Ruskin's *Rain in the Mountains*.

6.6. 1994

Dear Ruskin

Your sweet thought in having sent to me Rain in the Mountains is mush appreciated. I read one third at a sitting. As our hearts are in the mountains and your head, heart and body are physically and spiritually present there in the changing seasons in the Himalayas, I share with you your tendernesses. I am reviewing it for TRIBUNE

With warm regards,

Uncle Mulk

he flipped through the pages of that revered journal—the one and only family magazine of the 1950s, the gateway to literary success—edited by a quirky Irishman, Shaun Mandy.

And there it was—the first part of *The Room on the Roof*, that naive, youthful novel on which he had toiled for a couple of years. It had lively, evocative illustrations by Mario Miranda, who wasn't much older than him, and a picture of the young author, looking gauche and gaunt and far from intellectual.

He waved the magazine in front of Mr. Gupta. 'My novel!' he told him. 'In this and the next five issues!'

Mr. Gupta wasn't too impressed. 'Well, I hope circulation won't drop,' he said. 'And you should have sent them a better photograph.'

Expansively, Ruskin bought a third copy.

'Circulation is going up!' said Mr. Gupta with a smile.

The bazaar was slowly coming to life. Spring was in the air, and there was a spring in Ruskin's step as he sauntered down the road. He wanted to tell the world about his triumph, but was the world listening? He had no mentors in the sleepy little town. There was no one to whom he could go and say: 'Look what I've done. And it was all due to your encouragement. Thanks!'

There had been no one to encourage or help him, neither then nor in the distant past. The members of the local cricket team, to which he belonged, would certainly be interested, and one or two would certainly exclaim: '*Shabash!* Now you can get us some new pads and a set of balls!' And there were other friends who would demand a party at the *chaat* shop, which was fine, but would any of them read his novel? Readers were not exactly thick on the ground, even in those pre-television, pre-computer days. But perhaps one or two would read it, out of loyalty.

And he needed sustenance, for in a place like Dehra in the mid-fifties, literary influences were few and far between.

By day, he lived for his friendships and affairs; by night, he lived for his books and writing.

Home alone.

In *Coming Home to Dehra*, Ruskin recalls arriving at Dehra as a young lad and waiting for someone to turn up at the station to fetch him...

Coming Home to Dehra

The faint queasiness I always feel towards the end of a journey probably has its origin in that first homecoming after my father's death ...

... As the train drew into Dehra, I looked out of the window to see if there was anyone on the platform waiting to receive me. The station was crowded enough, as most railway stations are in India, with overloaded travellers, shouting coolies, stray dogs, stray station-masters.... Pandemonium broke loose as the train came to a halt and people debouched from the carriages. I was thrust on the platform with my tin trunk and small attache case. I sat on the trunk and waited for someone to find me.

Slowly the crowd melted away. I was left with one elderly coolie who was too feeble to carry heavy luggage and had decided that my trunk was just the right size and weight for his head and shoulders. I waited another ten minutes, but no representative of my mother or stepfather appeared. I permitted the coolie to lead me out of the station to the tonga stand ...

The Night Train to Delhi

'To be unconcerned about a desired good is probably the only way to possess it.'

The three years in Dehra were difficult ones. In his age group, anyone who wanted to do anything worthwhile was moving away from the 'slump the town was going through'. He too had to move on to a big city to look for a regular job.

In Delhi, initially he stayed in Rajouri Gardens with his mother and stepfather and then East Patel Nagar when they moved house. It was not easy and in the first year he had no job. But soon he started working for CARE (the Cooperative for American Relief Everywhere), an international relief agency. The job took him from one refugee camp to another—from the Tibetan settlement camps in Mussoorie, Darjeeling and Dalhousie to Bylakuppa, Mysore. He would write reports to the CARE headquarters to help channel funds to the right places.

From 1959 to 1963, Ruskin wrote travelogues, essays, and stories for children. His job left him with very little time to launch into longer manuscripts, so he would continue recording his impressions in his journals. Years later, he would dip into them for material to bring alive the times gone by. But this was a time of waiting, of soaking in that 'great greyness' called India.

FACING PAGE:

Back in Delhi.

After spending three difficult years in Dehra, Ruskin decided to come to Delhi looking for a job. Here he is on Delhi's Ridge Road at the time he was writing *Delhi is Not Far.*

Impressions of his life in the midst of a large Punjabi family—Bhabhiji, Kamal and his brother Jugal, and a host of others—populated the pages of the now-defunct Blackwood's Magazine, that great publishing house, which in its heyday, provided invaluable support to struggling writers from Walter Scott to Joseph Conrad.

It was during his years in Delhi that Ruskin met Anil Chopra (Bhabhiji's grandson), whom he shepherded through school and medical college. It was here that he fell in love with Sushila.

'Then, there was Sushila. She was about eighteen and I about thirty. She was the only girl I loved for more than six months! In fact in her case it was just over a year. I used to put her name on these books, the ones she said she liked, but I never noticed her reading them. Perhaps if she had married me, she would have read them. She was pretty, nice, and gentle. She shared her *jamuns* with me. A particular kind of girl that I always had a great weakness for. Darkish—like a deer. I hesitate to talk about this sweet and lovely girl, and you can read all about my infatuation in my story *Love is a Sad Song*. I believe she is well and happy somewhere in the wilds of West Delhi, blessed with five or six children. As I said, at the end of my story, I may have stopped loving you but I haven't stopped loving the days I loved you.'

The early sixties saw a clutch of short stories like *The Crooked Tree* and *Delhi is Not Far*. Ruskin's interest in impoverished neighbourhoods in small-town India comes to the fore in *Pipalnagar*—a world peopled by the simple folk—Deep Chand, the barber; Aziz, the *kabari*; Suraj, the hawker of knick-knacks; Pitamber, the rickshaw-wala; and Kamla, the prostitute.

'There is not exactly despair, but resignation, an indifference to both living and dying,' says Ruskin.

Once settled in Delhi, Ruskin made forays into nearby towns which come to life in his collection of essays *Strange Men, Strange Places*—short biographies of those early free-booters of the Raj, those swashbuckling, fortune-hunters intent on making good. In the Preface, he writes: 'Those odd, colourful (and admittedly not very "great") soldiers of fortune—mostly Europeans—who strutted across the Indian subcontinent during the eighteenth and nineteenth centuries and fought not for their country, nor for the East India Company, nor even their paymasters—at least, not for long but for their own hand, for their own

Where art thou, Sushila?

Ruskin wrote of his feelings for Sushila in *Love is a Sad Song.*

Love is a Sad Song

... I whispered to you, 'Sushila, there has never been anyone I've loved so much. I've been waiting all these years to find you. For a long time I did not even like women. But you are so different. You care for me, don't you?'

You nodded in the darkness. I could see the outline of your face in the faint moonlight that filtered through the skylight. You never replied directly to a question. I suppose that was feminine quality; coyness, perhaps.

'Do you love me, Sushila?'

No answer.

'Not now. When you are a little older. In a year or two.'

Did she nod in the darkness or did I imagine it?

'I know it's too early,' I continued. 'You are still too young. You are still at school. But already you are much wiser than me. I am finding it too difficult to control myself, but I will, since you wish it so. I'm very impatient, I know that, but I'll wait for as long as you make me—two or three or a hundred years. Yes, Sushila, a hundred years!'

Ah, what a pretty speech I made! Romeo could have used some of it; Majnu, too.

SADAR-I-RIYASAT.

Hari Niwas,
Jammu Tawi.

March 15, 1961.

My dear Mr. Bond,

This is just to let you know that I have been an interested reader of your 'Random Reflections ever since this feature was started in the Hindustan Times Sunday Magazine. As you perhaps know, I am myself an occasional contributor to this supplement.

I particularly liked your reflections published last Sunday on the forest pool of your childhood, and also thought that your short story was excellent. It struck me, however, that the title of the story was inappropriate, as it did not suggest the haunting and tender motif of the work.

I am a fairly frequent visitor to Delhi. Perhaps we may meet when I am there next.

Yours sincerely,

Karan Singh

YUVARAJ.

Mr. Ruskin Bond,
C/O The Hindustan Times,
Connaught Place,
New Delhi.

enrichment, for their own greater glory—and sometimes, simply because they liked fighting.'

'It isn't enough to read and re-write what you read,' says Ruskin. ' Once I got to a city where history was made, I would visit the churches, the cantonments, and the cemeteries to see for myself what it must have been like. History is best enjoyed by visiting the scene of actual events, and allowing the imagination to wander back and forth in time.'

It was during one of these forays some 250 miles from Delhi to Shahjehanpur (where Ruskin's father was born) that the turbulent days of 1857 came alive and the first draft of his novel *A Flight of Pigeons*, began to take shape. Years later, it was published in the November 1975 issue of *Imprint* magazine. The story remains, perhaps intentionally, lean on facts but brings out the essential goodness of human nature, especially in stressful times. Maybe it is Ruskin's own double inheritance that helps him bring out the ironic circumstances in which the Labadoors find themselves: they are a part of the European community only until the freedom fighters storm Shahjehanpur. And this very fact puts their lives at risk. But their Indian background comes to the fore as both the Hindus and Muslims give them shelter while the storm rages on outside.

Ismat Chugtai chanced upon the story, liked it, and showed it to filmmaker Shyam Benegal who offered Ruskin ten thousand rupees for the film rights. Later the film was produced by Shashi Kapoor, and called *Junoon*.

Fan mail.

A letter from Yuvraj Karan Singh expressing his desire to meet Ruskin. Amidst other things, Ruskin also wrote *Random Reflections* for the *Hindustan Times* Sunday Magazine for a living.

Back to the Hills of Home

6

'Perhaps a kindly wave will wash me ashore again, and someone else will pick me up.'

By the end of 1963, Ruskin had had his fill of big city life. He gave up his job in Delhi and moved to the foothills of Mussoorie, near his beloved Dehra. 'I was tired of a desk job. It could well have taken away my freedom and I could well have lost my dream of becoming a full-time writer,' he reminisces. But it was time to move on, flee the snares of the world.

'Mussoorie was a relatively inexpensive hill station in those days. It hadn't yet become a rich man's playground. I wasn't attracted to the town with its hammered biscuit-tin roofs, but there were hills, forests and simple villages nearby. I've had five addresses here, moving around from one ridge to the other, from single rooms to two or three at best—never more than that. Only in 2002 would I finally own the rooms I would live in.'

The hills were kind from the beginning and Ruskin began writing for children only after he came to live in the hills. He rented a small cottage on the outskirts of the hill station. Today, most hill station houses are for the affluent, but twenty-five years ago they were places where people of modest means could live quite cheaply. Mussoorie had very few cars and everyone walked from one place to another. Ruskin's cottage was on the edge of

FACING PAGE:

A family at last. Ruskin holds Prem Singh and Chandra's sons, Suresh who did not make it beyond the age of two, and Rakesh in his arms. Prem was only sixteen years old when he first arrived at Ruskin's house looking for his uncle and a job.

Prem and Chandra. The couple photographed at Maplewood Lodge in 1971. Thirty-three years later, Prem and his family are still looking after Ruskin.

the oak and maple forest and he spent nearly a decade in it, most of it happy, writing stories, essays, poems and books for children.

'I think this had something to do with Prem's children,' he says. Prem and his wife had taken on the responsibility of looking after the house and sorting out practical matters (Ruskin remains clueless about fuses, clogged cisterns, leaking gas cylinders, ruptured water pipes, tin roofs that blow away when there's a storm, and the do-it-yourself world of small-town India). They made it possible for him to write. Their sons Rakesh and Mukesh, and daughter Savitri (Dolly) grew up in Maplewood Lodge and then in other houses when they moved.

It was but natural for Ruskin to grow attached to them and become a part of the family, an adopted

grandfather. For Rakesh he wrote a story about a cherry tree that had difficulty in growing up; for Mukesh, who liked upheavals, he wrote a story about an earthquake and put him in it; and for Savitri he wrote rhymes and poems.

'The first year, I was in Oaklands Cottage, above the Wynberg School gate. I had rented the place from Mrs. Hathisingh, the old battle-axe whom I had met because she was my mother's friend. Both bred dogs, but hers were of dubious origin. She once fought a ten-year court case against a woman from Calcutta who had sued her for selling her a golden cocker spaniel, which after two or three baths had gone white! Mrs Hathisingh was most unattractive, and the ugliest woman you could possibly

The grandchildren. Mukesh, Savitri and Rakesh during a picnic at Wolfsbun, an old ruin. Ruskin wrote *Cherry Tree* for Rakesh.

imagine. I still can't figure out why men were so attracted to her. Very dominating. You had old Verma, only too willing to do her bidding. You had J.J. Singh and Ram Swarup. Old Col. Powell used to call her '*Neela Rani*' or the Blue Queen and it had more than one connotation to it. I remember when she died, this guy from Saharanpur turned up and paid for her funeral and vanished. Then there was that Station House Officer of Police...

'I don't think it was her sex appeal. I think she was a blackmailer who would get them to do her odd favours. After all, I was just living across the wall from her. Occasionally, she would peep over to see what was happening on my side of the wall. Young girls coming over constantly from one house to another. I put her in *Axe for the Rani.*'

It was here that Ruskin met Mrs. Sharma, a lecturer in English at one of the universities.

'"Hello!" she said to me, "You're Ruskin Bond!" Even in those pre-television days, people would occasionally recognize me and ask me to come over for lunch or dinner. And with her, it wasn't just a question of which daughter would be right for me. She wasn't just a matchmaker; she was a match fixer! And "fixed" all these matches for her daughters in the end. Asked me to come and stay as her guest. A real *phuljhari* she was. She had been widowed—her husband had died young. Her eldest daughter was from her first marriage. This one had gone to London and become a doctor there. Had a bit role in a film. Nothing to look at but a good-natured girl. Strong-willed with a mind of her own, assertive. She would always do her own thing. She smoked. She drank. She wanted to be a man. I don't know what her would-be husband saw in her. I think the

For children.

The hills inspired Ruskin to start writing stories for children.

In Oaklands Cottage.

Ruskin in Mrs Hathisingh's house in Mussoorie, providing the finishing touches to a story.

mother *phasaoed* him. She was a very jolly person. Good to chat and laugh with. The second daughter was pretty and sexy and the third was also very pretty and good-looking. Later, she married a film star, presumably is still married to him. This girl was very pretty. I had only known her two days and she was kissing me, wrapping me in her arms. A very passionate girl but she put me off a couple of weeks later by showing me her earlier love letters that various boyfriends had written to her. I'm going back to 1963-64 when I was just thirty, a slim and eligible bachelor or so I thought! They don't wrap me in their arms any more...

'I met them during my days in Oaklands Cottage, at Mrs. Hathisingh's house; Mrs. Sharma owned a house that has now vanished. She had probably inherited it. Those cane chairs in my sitting room, which I have even today, solid ones, she gave them to me. They are a constant reminder of her. Amazing how they made those chairs!

'In the neighbourhood lived the Ramadevi School Principal, Mr. Malhotra, who invited me to see his roses. Yes! He had this great rose garden. But I had

gone to see him to try and get Kamal admitted into Class X. He had never cleared any exams before that. I admired the roses and on the strength of that he gave Kamal admission. In those days, all it took was my saying: "Your roses are nice!" Admissions are more difficult these days.'

Ruskin has always had a penchant for falling in love with nurses—he goes to the hospital for a check-up and comes out five days later! Fortunately all the nurses with whom he becomes infatuated end up marrying doctors. Just as well.

Did he ever regret not marrying?

'I have no regrets about staying single. Marriage is a fine institution, I'm sure but basically I would hate to give up the independence I've enjoyed for the greater part of my life. I'm scared of being mothered or fussed over by some large imposing female. There's always Prem and his family, and they've looked after me like no one has been looked after before.'

And the family has been with Ruskin, living in rented houses or flats, till date. Whether it was a single-room, or two or three rooms Ruskin's address was always changing. Maplewood Lodge was an ideal place for a writer. At 6000 feet above sea level, the French windows opened out into the forest. 'When I pushed one open, the forest seemed to rush in upon me. The maples, oaks, rhododendrons and an old walnut, moved closer... Yes! It was a timeless sort of place,' says Ruskin.

'Over the years, I changed houses many times. Some were more congenial than others for writing. At Maplewood Lodge, where I lived until 1975, I wrote many of my early children's books—*Angry River* and *The Blue Umbrella,* to mention two of the most successful ones.'

Of course, the first few years were a struggle against all odds. Money was not plentiful, but Ruskin had no extravagant taste. There was always enough for his simple, unworldly needs. Things have not been very different during the many years in the hill station. The hills continue to be magical though hill stations today are tawdry, tatty places, Mussoorie being no exception. Tourism and private schools seem to have become its *raison d'être*. The odd writer who has come by this way has usually hurried on elsewhere. Ruskin stayed on because of his personal relationships. It had little to do with his writing, though he loves to sit in the shade of a friendly chestnut tree, notebook on his knee, he can write just as well in a crowded railway compartment or a seedy hotel veranda—and has frequently done so.

I first met Ruskin in 1969 in Maplewood Lodge. In the local college, I had heard of 'The sahib who writes all day' and imagined him to be like Phantom—the ghost who walks all night. So I wasn't surprised when I walked down a rubble-strewn path leading to the cottage and heard a voice exclaim: 'Ten years old and pregnant again!' The writer was chiding Toffee, his pet dog. By now, he had already become known around our little hill station for being a sort of Dr. Dolittle, taking his dog to the vet in a pram or listening patiently to everyone's story—from the baker complaining of poor yeast to the milkman's tale of a bad monsoon.

In July 1973, R.V. Pandit, publisher of *Imprint* magazine wrote in the editorial: 'I have a confession to make—from March 1968 this magazine has been run by remote control from abroad. I have a guilt to own; I have been able to spend only less and less time on *Imprint.* And

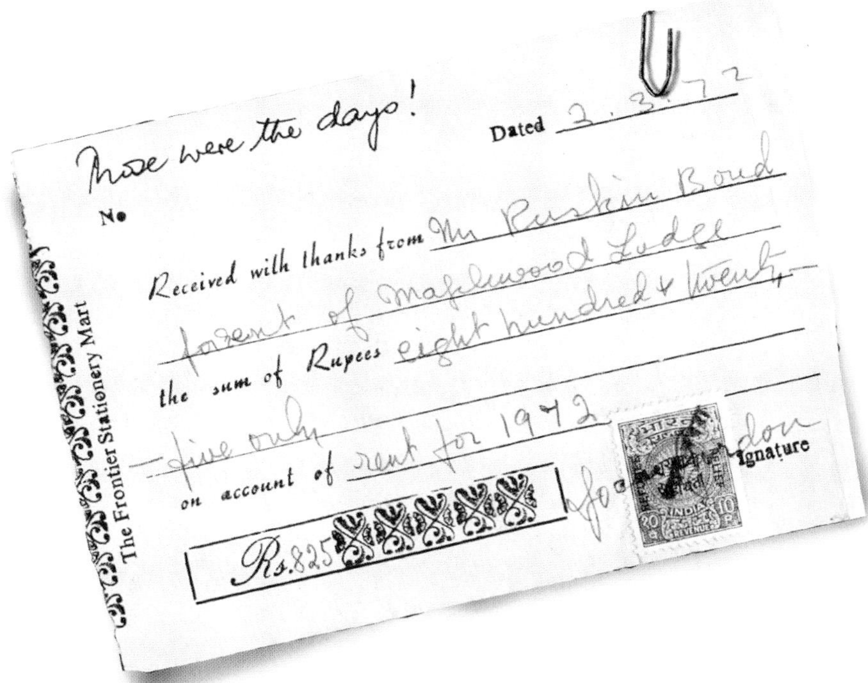

Those were the days!

No

Dated 3.3.72

Received with thanks from Mr Ruskin Bond for rent of Maplewood Lodge

the sum of Rupees eight hundred & twenty-five only

on account of rent for 1972

Signature

Rs.825

The Frontier Stationery Mart

this neglect—steadily gaping from the pages of this magazine—is giving you all, our ever-patient readers, an unfair deal.

Those were the days.

Ruskin's rent receipt from the owner of Maplewood Lodge.

'To remedy this situation, I have appointed Ruskin Bond, the novelist and short-story writer, Managing Editor of *Imprint*. Mr. Bond, whose work is known for its warmth and humanity, is already known to our readers. Mr. Bond will be responsible for fiction in the magazine.'

It was around this time that Bill Aitken first met Ruskin. In a letter to me, Bill recalls that meeting: 'When I first met Ruskin at Maplewood Lodge in the 1970s I was dressed in the robes of an ashram acolyte who had decided the religious life wasn't for him. Whereas the rest of polite Mussoorie society recoiled at the prospect of a hippie in their midst, Ruskin showed an almost maternal protectiveness towards him. It was clear from day one that he was fiercely committed to the rights of the underdog.

FACING PAGE:

Liberty, equality, fraternity.

Nothing in life is worth compromising one's principles, believes Ruskin firmly.

'I recall several instances of how he stood up for the poor man at the mercy of the privileged. In Landour, where the bungalows were owned largely by rich seasonal residents from the plains, Ruskin emerged as something of a Garhwali folk-hero by standing up for the locals' rights. On one occasion he had a face-off with an eccentric professor whose residence at a British university may have accounted for the colonial instinct to belabour his sweeper with his own *jharoo*. Ruskin has a pugnacious side to him and his threat to belabour the errant professor in turn was sufficiently meaningful for this bully to desist.'

On another level, affirms Bill, Ruskin believed in the importance of symbolic justice—to remind the exploiter (who thought he had got away with his injustice by economic or intellectual superiority) that cleverness is no substitute for fairness if you wish to become an accepted part of a community. The offender might wake up to find a window-pane of his vehicle cracked overnight from a stone 'dislodged' from the hillside above, a reminder that those who visit the mountains on four wheels should be alive to the feelings of whose who go around on their own two feet.

'It is difficult to make Ruskin really angry but when fully outraged the consequences can be spectacular,' writes Bill. On the occasion of a birthday party at Maplewood Lodge an uninvited whippersnapper tried to become familiar with Ruskin's lady guest of honour. To settle his hash, Ruskin opened the upstairs casement and seizing the offender bodily, threatened to throw him out of the window. Thus while concerned about the right of the underdog Ruskin was even-handed and would not allow the protocol of proper respect to be abused.

Bill also believes that Ruskin's essentially sympathetic nature altered a lot of destinies. He was generous to a fault with handouts to both deserving and undeserving cases. And this was all the more remarkable when as a freelancer he was living from hand to mouth.

'When I first met him at Maplewood Lodge he had staying with him a clutch of young pupils he was helping through Wynberg Allen School, a considerable financial burden.

'Having eschewed the ashram life I was badly in need of an occupation and Ruskin immediately came to my rescue by suggesting I help him with the editorial chores he had taken on with *Imprint*, a monthly magazine of literary content. I was given the job of retrieving from Ruskin's wastepaper basket those articles he had rejected. Typically he was too kind-hearted and wanted every budding writer to be given a second chance. As a fallout of reading rejected scripts I gained the confidence to start writing myself. Thereafter the fact that other hands rejected most of my early articles was like water off a duck's back.

'As my literary guru Ruskin had introduced me to one of the would-be writer's most crucial requirements—the ability to be objective in assessing the worth of one's own words.'

There was one particular contributor who never gave up inspite of repeated rejections. His unreadable magnum opus titled *India Good, Everybody King* was dutifully submitted every month, and followed up by personal visits by the author, a serving police officer. Ruskin had to use all his diplomatic tact to fend him off. Editing is more than just correcting proofs!

Down memory lane. With Prem and Toffee outside Maplewood Lodge in 1971. Toffee's brother Pickles was snapped up by a leopard just outside the kitchen at Maplewood Lodge.

Around the time of his stint with *Imprint*, a sixteen-year-old Prem Singh came into his life.

'He had come to the house asking after his uncle who was working for me. He stood on the landing outside the kitchen door. A tall boy, dark, with good teeth and brown deep-set eyes, dressed smartly in white drill—his only change of clothes—looking for a job. I liked the look of him.'

'I already have someone working for me,' Ruskin told him.

'Yes, Sir. He's my uncle. But he says you can find a job for me.'

'I'll try. Have you come from your village?'

'Yes! Yesterday I walked ten miles to Pauri. There I took a bus.'

'Sit down. Your uncle will make some tea.'

He sat down on the steps, removed his white Keds, and wriggled his toes. He was unusually clean for a hill boy. And taller than most.

'Do you smoke?' Ruskin asked.

'No, Sir.'

'It's true,' said his uncle, 'he does not smoke. All my nephews smoke but this one, he is a little peculiar, he does not smoke—neither bidi nor hookah.'

'Do you drink?'

'It makes me sick.'

'Do you take *bhang*?'

'No, Sahib.'

'You have no vices. It's unnatural.'

'He is unnatural, Sahib,' said his uncle.

'Does he chase girls?'

'They chase him, Sahib.'

'So he left the village and came looking for a job.' Ruskin looked at Prem. Prem grinned, then looked away, and began rubbing his feet.

'Your name is...?'

'Prem Singh.'

'All right, Prem, I will try to do something for you.'

Ruskin did not see Prem for a couple of weeks and forgot about finding him a job. But when he met Prem again on the road to the bazaar, Prem told him that he had got a temporary job in the Survey, looking after the surveyor's tents, and would be going to Rajasthan the following week.

Prem came from the hills where every family has a few terraced fields, narrow and stony, usually perched on a hillside above a stream or river. They grow rice, barley, maize, potatoes—just enough to live on. Even if their produce is sufficient for marketing, the absence of roads makes it difficult to get the produce to the market towns. There is no money to be earned in the villages, and money is needed for clothes, soap, medicines, and to recover family jewellery from moneylenders. So the young men leave their villages in search of work, and to find work they must go to the plains. The lucky ones get into the army. Others enter domestic service or take up jobs at garages, hotels, wayside teashops, and schools.

In Mussoorie the large number of schools that employ cooks and bearers are a key draw. But when Prem had arrived, these schools had nothing to offer. He had been to the recruiting centre at Roorkee, hoping to get into the army, but they found a deformity in his right foot—the result of a broken bone after a landslip had carried him away one dark monsoon night.

He came to the house to inform his uncle about the job and say goodbye. 'Well,' thought Ruskin to himself, 'there goes another nice person I probably won't see again; another ship passing in the night, the friendly twinkle of its light soon vanishing in the darkness.'

A year went by, then Prem returned, somewhat thinner and darker, still smiling and still looking for a job. Ruskin found him a job in the nearby school. The headmaster's wife needed a cook.

Three days later the headmaster's wife met Ruskin on the road and started gushing all over him. She was the sort who gushed.

Prem looked cheerful enough when he came to see Ruskin on his off day.

Home is where the heart is.

A photograph of Prem's wife Chandra, with their son Mukesh when he was perhaps nine or ten. Today Mukesh is a strapping young lad, and an important member of Ruskin's family of eleven.

'How are you getting on?' Ruskin asked.

'Lovely,' he said, using his mistress's favourite expression.

'What do you mean "Lovely"? Do they like your work?'

'The memsahib likes it. She strokes me on the cheek whenever she enters the kitchen. The sahib says nothing. He takes medicines after every meal.'

'Did he always take medicines—or only now that you are doing the cooking?'

'I am not sure, I think he has always been sick.'

Sitting under the cherry tree, its leaves just beginning to turn yellow, Ruskin gazes across the valley to where Prem moves about in the garden. He recalls some of the nicest things about Prem. They come to him in no particular order—random images flitting across the screen of memory: Prem rocking his infant son to sleep, crooning to him, passing his large hand gently over the child's curly head...Prem following him down to the police station when Ruskin was arrested during the infamous Emergency for writing an allegedly 'obscene' story published in a Bombay magazine. (It was a non-bailable offence, but the lawyer, the ever-resourceful N.P. Jain had it converted to a bailable one with the full cooperation of the local police. And Sudhakar Misra, a colleague from the Degree College, and I stood bail. But

until the case was finally decided in his favour, it meant endless visits to the court in far-off Bombay.)

'Of course there were times when Prem could be infuriating, stubborn, deliberately pig-headed, sending me little notes of resignation, but I never found it difficult to overlook these little acts of self-indulgence. He had brought much more love and laughter into my life, and what more could a lonely man ask for?' says Ruskin.

It was this stubborn streak that cut short Prem's stay in the headmaster's household. Mr. Good was tolerant enough. But Mrs. Good was one of those women who, when pleased with you, went out of her way to help, pamper and flatter, but when displeased, turned vindictive, seeking to harm or destroy. Mrs. Good sought power—over her husband, her dog, her favourite pupils, her servant.... She had absolute power over the husband and the dog, partial power over her slightly bewildered pupils and none at all over Prem who missed the subtleties of her designs upon his soul. He did not respond to her mothering, or to the way in which she tweaked him on the cheeks, brushed against him in the kitchen and made remarks about his good looks and physique. Memsahibs, he knew, were not for him. So he kept a stony face and went about his duties diligently. She, however, felt slighted. Soon enough, her like turned to

Family bonds.
Prem with his son Rakesh at Maplewood Lodge when the family was just starting to grow.

With Mukesh in 1980.

Since Mukesh was very fond of upheavals, Ruskin wrote the story of an earthquake for him.

dislike, and she began making disparaging remarks about his looks, his clothes, his manners. She found fault with his cooking. No longer was it 'Lovely'. She even accused him of taking away the dog's meat and giving it to a poor family living on the hillside—no more heinous a crime could be imagined!

Once, Mr. Good threatened Prem with dismissal. So Prem became stubborn. The following day he withheld the dog's food altogether, threw it down the *khud* where innumerable strays seized upon it. Then he went off to the movies, to watch the latest Laurel and Hardy. That was the end of his job.

'I'll have to go home now,' he told Ruskin. 'I won't get another job in this area. The memsahib will see to that.'

'Stay a few days,' Ruskin said.

'I have only enough money to get home.'

'Keep it for going home. You can stay with me for a few days while you look around. Your uncle won't mind sharing his food with you.'

His uncle did mind.

He did not like the idea of working for his nephew as well; it seemed to him no part of his duties. And he was apprehensive about Prem taking away his job.

So Prem stayed no longer than a week before returning to his village.

Several months went by before Ruskin saw Prem again. His uncle told

Ruskin that he had taken up a job in Delhi. There was an address. It did not, however, seem complete.

And then the uncle decided to move on. He had found a better-paid job in Dehra and was anxious to be off.

For the next six months Ruskin lived in the cottage without any help. He did not find this difficult since he was used to living alone. It wasn't service that he needed but companionship. It was very quiet in the cottage. Perhaps the ghosts of residents long dead were sympathetic but unobtrusive.

During the rains, watching the trees dripping and the mist climbing the valley, Ruskin wrote a great deal of poetry. But poetry didn't bring much money, and funds were low. And then, just as Ruskin was wondering if he would have to give up his freedom and take up a job again, a foreign publisher bought the paperback rights of one of his children stories, *Angry River*. And he was free to live and write as he pleased—for another three months or so. That was in winter, and to celebrate the occasion, he took a long walk through the Landour Bazaar and up the Tehri road. It was a good day for walking, and by the time he returned to the outskirts of the town, it was dark. Someone stood waiting for him on the road above the cottage. Ruskin hurried past him, then walked back to the shadows where the youth stood and saw that it was Prem.

'Prem!' Ruskin said. 'Why are you sitting out here, in the cold? Why did you not go to the house?'

'I went, Sir, but there was a lock on the door. I thought you had gone away.'

'And you were going to remain here, on the road?'

'Only for tonight. I would have gone down to Dehra in the morning.'

'Come, let's go home. I have been waiting for you. I looked for you in Delhi, but could not find the place where you were working.'

'I have left them now.'

'And your uncle has left me. So will you work for me now?'

'For as long as you wish.'

'For as long as the gods wish.'

And with that one small step, a new journey had begun.

That was more than thirty years ago, and Prem and his wife Chandra and their three children are still with Ruskin. So are Rakesh and Mukesh's wives, and Rakesh's three children and Mukesh's son.

Ruskin has come a long way from the trying times of the first ten years as a writer. There were very few outlets for his work in those days. The publishing boom was still twenty years away. On one occasion, he was saved (or so he thought) by a 'far-out' ex-hippie and ex-Hollywood scriptwriter who decided he would produce a children's film based on one of Ruskin's stories *Big Business*. It was a pleasant little story, and all would have gone well had the producer not returned from some high-altitude poppy fields in a bit of a trance and failed to notice that his leading lady was in the family way. Although the events of the story all took place in a single day, the film itself took about four months to complete, with the result that her figure altered considerably from scene to scene until, by late evening of the same day, she was displaying all the glories of imminent motherhood. The film, of course, was never released.

Ruskin has had a fair-share of tacky publishers down the years. One paid in cash, giving him two five hundred-rupee notes—one damaged and the other fake. Another feigned a heart attack when reminded of royalties. And there is one who takes him out for dinner, once a year. Just the other day a would-be publisher sent a one-rupee money order to check if the address he had was right. Another new entrant into the world of publishing wrote: 'Sir! We are entering the world of publishing. Please let us know what you do?'

And then there were personal losses.

On Christmas Eve in 1970, Ruskin's thirty-year-old half-brother Harold set out from Dehra in his father's car, to get to Delhi in time for a party at the Anglo-Indian Club. Although Harold was a good driver, having taken part in car rallies and other tests of speed and endurance, he had become a heavy drinker and was in no condition to undertake a long and arduous drive late at night all by himself. Near Mansurpur, apparently his car was crushed between two trucks that disappeared into the night. Harold was killed instantly, or so it appeared. No one ever learnt about the circumstances that led to the accident.

'What can one say about Harold?' says Ruskin ruefully. 'He was attractive to women, but they had a hard time looking after him. And he wrecked their lives in addition to his own.'

Harold and Ruskin's interests were very different, but they did not come in each other's way. Harold left Ruskin to his books and long walks; Ruskin left Harold to his motorcycles and dance parties.

In 1969 their mother died of breast cancer before Harold's fatal accident, so she was spared a double heartbreak—a few months later Ruskin's second half-brother Hansel too died in a motorcycle accident in 1971. Ironically, Hansel was the careful one who seldom took risks.

Ruskin's brother William left India for England in 1965, and finally settled in Canada. His sister Ellen lives with his stepsister Premela, on his father's RAF pension in Jullunder.

Tragedy struck again in 1976 when Prem's second born, the two-year-old Suresh, died of tetanus. The family was distraught and moved to Saket. The flat was owned by Mr. Puri, and stood on the bridal path to King Craig with the valley of the Doon stretched out below like a vast amphitheatre.

From Saket, Ruskin moved to Prospect Point, in Landour, beyond Sisters Bazaar. He had strange neighbours—from the lady who played the sitar while a forest fire raged around the house to the man who did acupressure till he rolled down the *khud* and had to be rushed to the Community Hospital, where acupressure didn't help him at all! But Prospect Point was too far from town and the school that Rakesh, then seven, went to.

So, in 1981 Ruskin moved down and rented Ivy Cottage. Here he lives happily with his large adoptive family—Prem and Chandra, their three children, two daughters-in-law, and four grandchildren. He prefers to see himself as a good football goalkeeper—one of the few accomplishments that he isn't quite modest about! And although his football-playing days ended when he left school, he has been a goalkeeper all his life—protecting home territory rather than being an aggressive goal-scorer or go-getter; in other words, a stout defender rather than a dashing, flashy centre-forward. An occasional high kick to feed the forwards can always be expected; the rest of the time he is happy to use his good reflexes to protect his loved ones, his way of life, and his privacy.

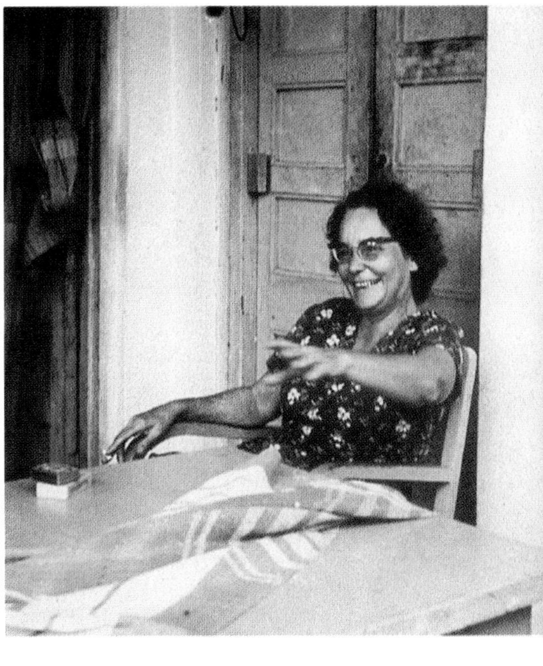

In 2002, the owners of Ivy Cottage finally managed to persuade Ruskin to buy the flat he had lived in for over twenty years. Although Ruskin prides himself on being able to write anywhere, he feels houses with a congenial atmosphere have worked wonders for his writing. And he is not talking about beautiful houses set against a picturesque landscape. Some of his best stories were written in a small flat overlooking Rajpur Road in Dehra. Similarly, *The Room on the Roof* was written in a tiny attic in London. He also started writing for children at Maplewood Lodge in Balahissar, and continues to do so in Ivy Cottage. Prolific as ever, Ruskin has lived in barren surroundings during his years in Delhi, and in the picturesque Prospect Point at the top of Landour where he says the wind and his neighbours used to irritate him. 'I never did anything of significance there.'

Remembrances. This was the last photograph of Ruskin's mother, taken in Delhi a few years before she passed away.

'Maplewood Lodge was down in the forest. The house was old and had a character of its own. Out of its French

The Olympia typewriter has been a companion Ruskin could always count on.

SCHOLASTIC

Great and grand. Ruskin plays great-grandfather to Shrishti, Rakesh's daughter, at Ivy Cottage.

windows, one could touch the trees. Ivy Cottage has no particular atmosphere but the clouds from my window give me messages I can't ignore. If I write my autobiography, it will, I think, be called *Writing For My Life*. Ever since I started freelancing, on my return from England in 1955, I have been writing in order to sustain the sort of life I like to lead—unhurried, even-paced, sensual, in step with the natural world, most at home with humble people. I have never aspired to cars, houses, or even furniture. Property is for the superstitious. I have no assets except the books I have written and the few that may still be lurking in the innermost recesses of my mind. "I give to the world that which is in my heart," wrote the composer Franz Schubert, and I have tried to do the same. Hopefully it will outlast the furniture. Yet there are times when I do love my art. And because I have loved it, I think I have been able to pass through life without being any man's slave or tyrant. I doubt if I have ever written a story or essay or workaday article unless I have really wanted to write it. And in this way I have probably suffered materially, because I have never attempted a blockbuster of a novel, or a biography of a celebrity, or a soap opera that goes on forever. The prospect of spinning out thousands of words of little or no consequence seems a dull and dreary way of earning a living.

'"Writing is easy," said Red Smith. "All you have to do is sit at

your typewriter till little drops of blood appear on your forehead." That's true for some of us. But I refuse to suffer. At the first sign of drops of blood or perspiration, I get up from my desk and do something totally different—make myself a sandwich, water my ferns, take a walk, or discuss politics with the milkman. If the writing isn't easy, if I'm not enjoying it, I know I'm better off doing something else. And yet writing is easy if I'm happy with my theme. Ask me to write a piece on petunias, and I'll turn out an enthusiastic essay on this underrated flower. I might even write a story about someone who grows petunias,

With the writer.
Admirers flock constantly to Ivy Cottage to meet Ruskin Bond, the writer. This particular group had come all the way from a school in Hyderabad to see him.

FACING PAGE:

Unanswered question.

'Why so much pride when a little humility can get us far more by way of love and peace and happiness?'

because such a person must obviously have sterling qualities. I might even delve into the love life of a petunia-grower because those who love flowers must, by their very nature, be loving, even sensual and passionate people, from *The Rose Garden* of Sa'adi to Wordsworth's field of golden daffodils. Of flowers, lovers, melons and moonbeams, I can write reams. But ask me to write the life story of a great leader or media tycoon or matchbox-maker, and I'm stumped and stymied. Those little drops of blood threaten to appear. I cannot breathe life into these subjects, noble though they might be. Their true personality, the essence of their natures somehow eludes me. It is not that they are too complicated, but rather that one has to peel off too many layers of protective armour to get at the flesh and blood that lies beneath the skin. Why is humility so hard to come by? Most religions teach the wisdom of humility, but who listens? We all know that life is finite, that human civilization, for what it's worth, is self-limiting. And yet the most educated of men will strut about their little world like actors on a stage; they assume the mantle of immortals, deluding themselves into thinking they are indispensable, until eventually they join all those other indispensables who have reached perfection in the form of dust or ashes.

'Why so much pride when a little humility can get us far more by way of love and peace and happiness? Better to efface yourself like the cricket that is heard but seldom seen than to flap your wings and crow like a cock before ending up as someone's *tandoori* dinner.

'Happiness is an elusive state of mind, not to be gained by clumsy pursuit. It is given to those who do not strive for it: to be unconcerned about a desired good is

probably the only way to possess it. "I enjoy life," said Seneca, "because I am ready to leave it." If we can disencumber ourselves of nine-tenths of our worldly goods, it should not be difficult to leave the rest behind. But it's amazing how most of us hang on to our bric-à-brac, hoping maybe that it will be treasured and valued by those who come after us... "How weary, stale, flat and unprofitable!" sighed Hamlet in another context, although he might well have been commenting on the values of our own time.'

Over the years, Ruskin has many times been bullied, pestered or simply harassed into writing Forewords and Introductions for budding writers, and often with hilarious results: an elderly gentleman, having written his first book called *The Maneater of Dogadda*, approached Ruskin to write an Introduction. The publishers got the captions mixed up as was evident when the book was released. On the cover was a picture of the dead leopard entitled 'Famous author Ruskin Bond' and the picture of a beaming Ruskin on the back cover had the legend, 'The Slain Maneater of Dogadda!'

Recently, Ruskin did a tongue-in-cheek Foreword for a book of little or no merit simply because the woman, a teacher, was harassing him in person and over the phone twice a day. So, one day he gave in and wrote a Foreword in which he refers to her work 'as an ornament of Indo-Anglian literature'. The school's stationery printers in Delhi were all set to print.

She called again: 'Mr. Bond! How do I get my book nominated for the Nobel Prize?'

'Just get your publishers to submit it on your behalf.'

'But what about the Booker Prize? My writing is better than Arundhati Roy's.'

'Well, for that you have to be published in the U.K.'

'How do I do that? My publisher doesn't have a branch in England, Mr. Bond!'

'Tell them to open one. And meantime, don't forget to submit it for the Nobel Prize!' he managed to mumble.

Another fan wrote: 'I want to be a writer like you, so that I can lie on the grass and do nothing.'

Lying on the grass and doing nothing is of course a wonderful occupation, but Ruskin did not survive as a freelance writer for over forty years simply by lying on the grass and counting ladybirds. If the grass is to mean anything, a time comes when you have to get up, brush the ladybirds off your shirt and trousers, and proceed to your desk to write, type or word-process all those ideas you get while sitting out there 'doing nothing'.

FACING PAGE:

The philosopher.

'If we can disencumber ourselves of nine-tenths of our wordly goods, it should not be difficult to leave the rest behind.'

Amongst Friends

7

'And yet, quite often,
I've had roses out of season.'

Around 1976, I bought a second-hand motorcycle from an ex-hippie. Ruskin was great at riding pillion. We would go all over town on it. It was great for our social life. On one such outing, after attending a friend's hilltop *bhang* party on Holi, Ruskin mistook a respectable old gentleman for a lady of easy virtue, and we had to leave in a hurry. But our genial publisher Pramod Kapoor who was also at that party, was in no hurry to leave with us as he sat propped up against some bolsters watching a one-day international. When our actor-friend Victor Banerjee (a soccer fan) disturbed the proceedings, lots of things hit the ceiling and Ruskin commemorated the incident in following limerick:

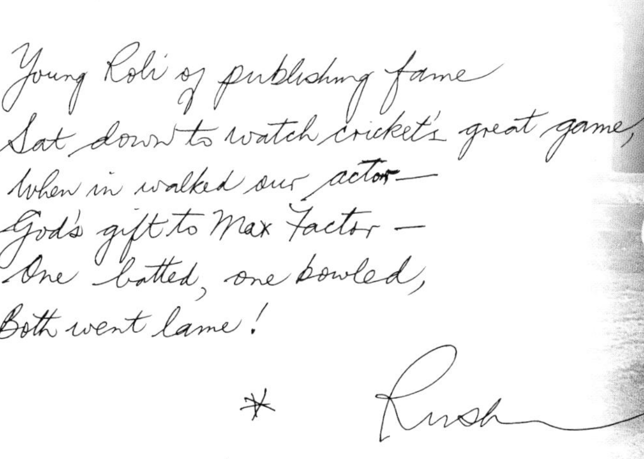
Young Roli of publishing fame
Sat down to watch cricket's great game,
When in walked our actor—
God's gift to Max Factor—
One batted, one bowled,
Both went lame!

* Ruskin

Landour

FACING PAGE AND BELOW:

The school of life.

The greatest tutor for Ruskin has been the school of life. Success sits gently on him till this day.

A neighbour and a friend.

With actor and close friend Victor Banerjee in Calcutta in 2002.

Some winters ago, we were sitting with Nandu Jauhar, the affable owner of the Savoy Hotel, sipping brandy in front of a crackling wood fire at Nandu's private sitting room at the Savoy. It was an idyllic scene, straight out of Dickens. You could say Ruskin was Pickwick, Nandu was Micawber, I was Sam Weller—each of us had something in common with these characters.

Nandu hadn't used the fireplace for some years, but since it was Christmas and bitterly cold outside, he thought it would be a good time for a blazing fire in an old-fashioned fireplace—a supreme indulgence.

And blaze it did! We hadn't enjoyed a really roaring fire in years. And the brandy was good too. So good that it took us some time to realize that those lovely crackling sounds were actually emanating from the roof as well as the fireplace. The chimney was on fire!

We ran outside to find flames leaping into the night sky. The chimney, unused and neglected for fifty years, was ablaze and sparks were flying in all directions. It was all hands on deck, or rather on the roof, and it was a sight to watch dear Nandu cavorting around with a bucketful of water. Ruskin dashed inside to make sure the brandy hadn't caught fire, poured himself a stiff one, and returned to join the firefighters, mainly the late-night kitchen staff, most of whom had been celebrating Christmas in their own way.

Luckily, the fire was brought under control before it could get anywhere near the Savoy's famous Writers' Bar.

Over the years, the Writers' Bar has been a place where we have met many interesting people: actors, authors, journalists, diplomats, drunks, cops and bureaucrats (serving, retired and on retreading).

Of course, a lot of people who enter the Writers' Bar look pretty far gone, and sometimes one has difficulty distinguishing the living from the dead. But the real ghosts are those who manage to slip away without paying for their drinks.

Ruskin doesn't have to slip away. In the ten or twelve years during which he has helped prop up the place, he has seldom paid for a drink. That's the kind of friend he has in Nandu. One won't find a harsh word about him in

Ruskin's writing. Perhaps Nandu decided long ago that Ruskin was an adornment to the bar, and that draped over a bar stool, he looked like Ray Miland in *The Lost Weekend*.

But how did the old Savoy bar come to be known as the 'Writers' Bar'? Well! Thereby hangs a tale!

For quite some time, Nandu had thought of naming it so. And it was rechristened after the following exchange:

'But to do that,' Ruskin said, 'you'd have to get a few writers in here, wouldn't you?'

'Well, you're one, aren't you? Don't you have any writer friends?'

'Hardly any. And the few I know are teetotallers. The Hemingway types are out of fashion.'

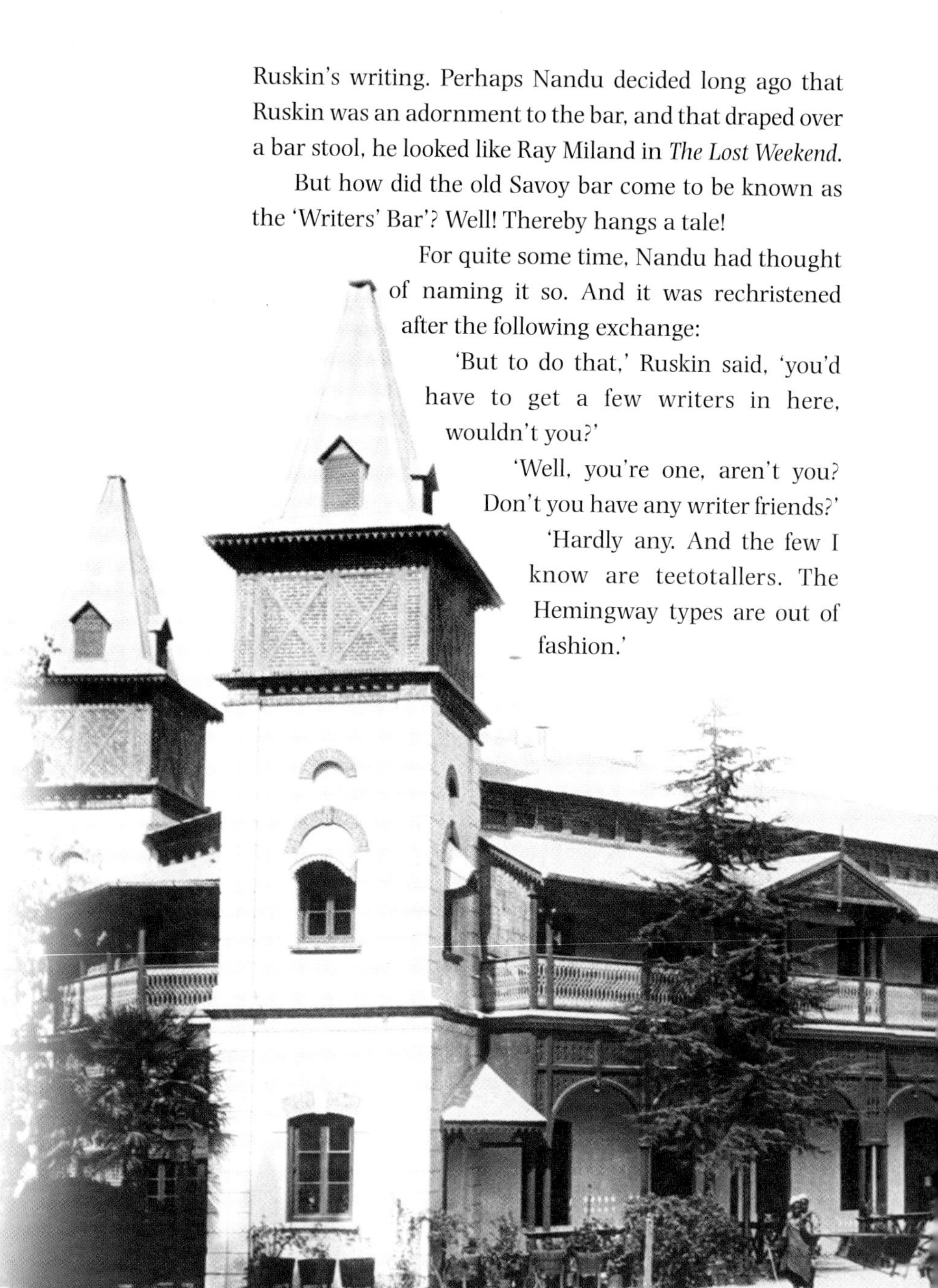

'Last year, when I was in Singapore,' said Nandu, 'I revisited the historic Raffles Hotel. It's about the same age as the Savoy—and they had a Writers' Bar with brass plaques on the walls stating that Somerset Maugham had been there, and Joseph Conrad, and Graham Greene.'

'All very sober people,' Ruskin remarked.

'Yes, but they stayed there, and they must have had the occasional drink at the Bar, even if it was only a *nimbu pani*.'

'Well, in the old days, the Savoy must have had the occasional writer staying here.'

'There was Pearl S. Buck. I still have her autograph in one of her books. She won the Nobel Prize, didn't she?'

'She did, but I doubt if she

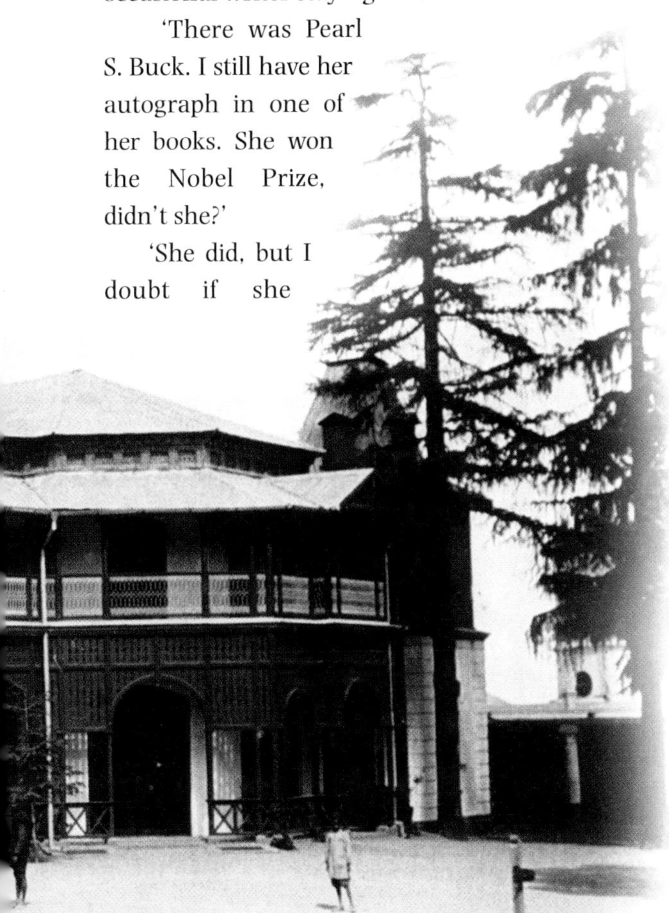

The Savoy.

With a little help from good friend Ruskin, Nandu Jauhar managed to get the Writers' Bar in place at the Savoy.

Amongst friends.

With old school friend Kasper Kirschner (left), now a senior scientist in Switzerland, and Her Highness Prithvi Bir Kaur of Jind (right) at Oakless Cottage.

frequented the bar. I believe she was the daughter of missionaries.'

'All the more reason to take to drink. In any case she must have looked in here from time to time. We'll put her name on a plaque.'

'All right. We've got Pearl S. Buck.'

'What about Rudyard Kipling? He must have stayed here.'

'My dear chap,' says Ruskin, 'the hotel opened in

1905. By that time Kipling had left India, never to return.'

'You're not being very helpful,' said Nandu. 'What about John Masters?'

'Quite possible,' said Ruskin. 'He served with a Gurkha regiment in Dehra. Must have come up the hill occasionally. Probably dropped in for a drink. Here or at the Charleville.'

'Forget about the Charleville, it burnt down years ago. We'll give John Masters a plaque. That's two we've got!'

'Why don't you look up the old hotel register?' Ruskin asked.

FACING PAGE:

The Landour Chakkar.

With Ganesh, Siddharth and Binita Thakur after a walk around the Landour Chakkar.

FACING PAGE:

A stroll in the hills. Ruskin takes writers and journalists around Landour during the first Writers' Retreat organized by Roli Books in 2001.

'The previous manager walked off with it,' said Nandu ruefully.

'Probably wanted Pearl S. Buck's autograph.'

'Who was that fellow who wrote about the separation bell? You know, the bell they used to ring at four every morning so that people could get back to their own rooms?'

'I've heard of the bell,' Ruskin said. 'But I can't remember the name.'

'Somerset Maugham?'

'I don't think he visited Mussoorie. It was a travel writer.'

'The Gantzers? Bill Aitken?'

'They are still alive. But if you ask them in for a drink, they might let you put their names up.'

'A free drink, you mean?' Nandu didn't look too happy.

'Naturally.'

'Let's stick to the dead. Pandit Nehru stayed here. He was a writer.'

'Yes, Nandu. But I don't think you'd have found him in the bar.'

'Sir Edmund Hillary?'

'Well, he wrote his autobiography. Probably stopped by for a drink after climbing the Everest.'

'All right, I've got it! Jim Corbett.'

'But he lived in Nainital,' Ruskin protested. 'I doubt if he ever came here.'

'His parents were married in Landour. You told me yourself. And he wrote that book, *The Maneater of Rudraprayag*. Rudraprayag is only eighty miles from here, as the crow flies.'

'All right, all right. And after shooting the maneater, Corbett tramped all the way to Mussoorie to have a refreshing beer at the Savoy. There was no motor road then, Nandu. He must have needed a drink badly.'

'It's possible. He used to walk great distances.'

'To shoot maneaters, not to drink beer. But let's give him a plaque, on the strength of his parents having been married in Mussoorie. Who do we have now?'

'Pearl S. Buck, John Masters, Jim Corbett!'

The plaques were prepared. The Writers' Bar was inaugurated in the spring of 2001. If any reader can come up with a suitable candidate for inclusion, he'll be entitled to a free drink.

Ruskin has been in Mussoorie for forty years now, and at long last, has a family of his own. I always tell him that he's lucky to have gone from being a bachelor to a grandfather without marriage in between! Travel writers Hugh and Colleen Gantzer describe their experience of knowing Ruskin as 'Bonding with the Best': 'Honestly what does one say about a friend? That we like him? That's obvious. That we value his friendship? We've known

Ruskin for more than three decades. Our son, who is a father today, was small enough then to be carried in a harness on our backs. On a clear Himalayan morning we walked down to Maplewood Lodge, knocked on a cottage door, and got to know Ruskin. We didn't realize it ourselves, at the time. But, in retrospect, it was clearly a turning point in our lives. We found ourselves talking seriously about making freelance writing a career. A few months later, we were no longer a serving Indian Naval family and had become freelance writers. So, perhaps, Ruskin was, in a way, responsible for what we do today.'

Today, Ruskin meets his friends at sundown for a sling or two. When I ask him whether he's ever been on the wagon, he tells me it was only when the doctor ordered abstinence. Otherwise there are few pleasures that would match the magic of sitting with friends by a fire, over a few 'snick-snacks' and a good conversation—a 'fellowship' reminiscent of the one Dr. Johnson shared with his friends.

With self-deprecating humour, he'll poke fun at his own absent-mindedness. On more than one occasion, in the throes of composition, he has dipped his pen into his teacup. He has turned up at parties on the wrong day, and posted letters without addresses. Once he even took a party of trekkers up the wrong valley, and they were lost in the mountains for days. Only the other day at the bank, instead of handing the cashier a cheque, he gave him an old *Imprint* rejection slip. The bank teller was not amused. 'It should teach me a lesson for being so liberal with rejection slips!' he smiles.

Today, Ruskin lives in simple, even austere conditions. Prem and the family have two small rooms; Ruskin has two small rooms. Books and a few chairs for the occasional visitor take up one of these. The other, smaller one, is his bedroom-cum-study. It is a bright and sunny room, and the windows open out to the mountains and valley. On the road below people and vehicles pass by.

Does Ruskin have any regrets?

He thinks long and hard: 'I would have liked to be kinder to some people, and tougher and more unyielding to others. It is the kind of regret that is common to most of us. But that apart, my failure to make it to Torquay United's football "B" team. I don't think there's much I can complain about.'

And what does he feel about his own writing?

Ruskin says gently: 'Amongst writers, I am not one of the big guns. I am not even a little gun. I prefer to see myself as just a small pebble lying on the beach. But I would like to think that I am a smooth, round, colourful pebble, and that someone will pick me up, derive a little pleasure from holding me, and possibly even put me in his or her pocket. And if one tires of me, one can always throw me back into the sea. Perhaps a kindly wave will wash me ashore again, and someone else will pick me up.'

Raki, Muki, Dolly...and now Siddharth, Shristhi, Gautam, Atish...they have grown up with Ruskin, they are with him now.... If he ever leaves this town for another place, they will go with him. If they grow up and go away, he will be near them. That's what love is all about. Being there always.

As he puts it: 'Most of my life I have given of myself, and in return I have received love in abundance. Life hasn't been a bed of roses. And yet, quite often, I've had roses out of season.'

The writer and his biographer.

Ruskin strikes a pose with Ganesh Saili, his biographer. Ruskin and Ganesh have known each other for over thirty years.

Epilogue

A friend of forty years, Ganesh Saili taught me how to drink and ride a motor-cycle. (But I don't drink on a motor-cycle.)

Everything I've learnt in life is from younger people.

Today, Ganesh drives around in his red Santro — sometimes with his family, sometimes with me, but more often with his Landour Labrador ~ a dog of indeterminate breed (but of course there's something to be said for character.)

His wife Abha and I are both suing him for a divorce settlement. She gets his camera. I get the Labrador. So much for love and loyalty!

Ganesh has two beautiful and

talented daughters, who have always been kind to me.

It's nice to have a home away from home. Ganesh and Abha's home has been there all these years, and I know it will always be there. We have walked down the steep and narrow lanes of Mussoorie for the better part of our lives. There have been good times and bad times, but the good times have predominated.

Ruskin

28/7/04

From Ruskin's Pen

1952-1955: Jersey, the Channel Islands

The Room on the Roof (based on 1951 Dehradun Journal, developed as his first novel).

Untouchable (a story), two or three lost stories, *Maharani* and talks on the BBC

1955-1958: Freelancing in Dehradun

Vagrants in the Valley (a sequel to *The Room on the Roof)*

Time Stops at Shamli

The Night Train at Deoli

The Eyes are Not Here (The Eyes Have It)

The Thief

The Big Race

Big Business

The Long Day

The Photograph

Somi's World Tour

The Tikki Eating Contest (lost)

Woman on Platform 8

The Fight

Calypso Christmas

1958-63: In Delhi

Grandfather's Private Zoo

The Hidden Pool

Delhi is Not Far (a novella)

A Flight of Pigeons

Strange Men, Strange Places

1964-1976: Maplewood and Saket

A Prospect of Flowers

The Leopard

Tiger in the Tunnel

He Said it with Arsenic

Cherry Tree

Binya Passes By

Love is a Sad Song

Blackwood & Christian Science Monitor (Essays and poems)

Children's Books in this Period:

Angry River

The Blue Umbrella

Night of the Leopard

Landour

Tales & Legends from India

The Road to the Bazaar

Getting Granny's Glasses

Tigers Forever

Dust on the Mountain

Ghost Trouble

Snake Trouble

Earthquake
Himalayan Tales
Rain in the Mountains
Strangers in the Night
When Darkness Falls
Landour Days
A Season of Ghosts
The India I Love
A Little Night Music (verse)
Ruskin Bond's Book of Nature
A Face in the Dark
Brief Lives
and many more...

Awards

John Llewellyn Rhys Award 1957 for The Room on the Roof

Sahitya Akademi Award 1993-94 for Our Trees Still Grow in Dehra

Padma Shri, 1999.

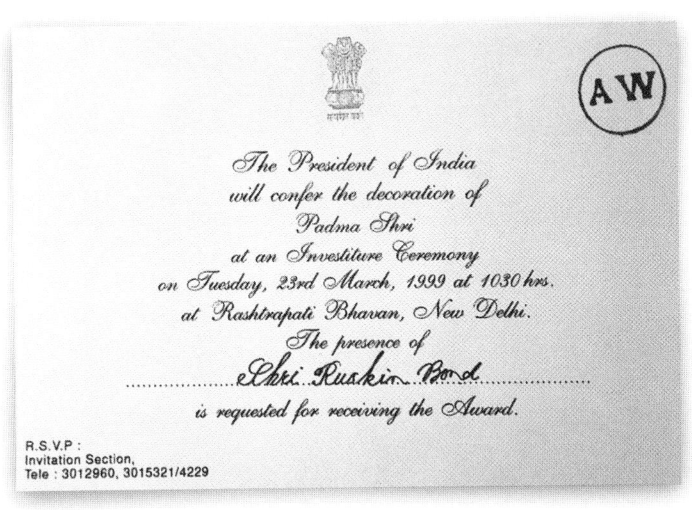

AW

The President of India
will confer the decoration of
Padma Shri
at an Investiture Ceremony
on Tuesday, 23rd March, 1999 at 1030 hrs.
at Rashtrapati Bhavan, New Delhi.
The presence of
Shri Ruskin Bond
is requested for receiving the Award.

R.S.V.P :
Invitation Section,
Tele : 3012960, 3015321/4229

COLOUR MAGAZINE

The Telegraph

8 DECEMBER 1991

THE OTHER BOND

BOOKS

Ruskin Bond as the perpetual adolescent of the hills

BOOKS

Natur

The work of

THE LITERARY LIFE

From Ruskin with love

His name may be Bond—but he prefers a typewriter to a Walther PPK, and bun-omelettes to Beluga

Unlike his fictional namesake, Mr Bond favours neither fast cars nor martinis (shaken, not stirred). The latter don't go down well with his ulcer and the former have no place in the tiny bylanes of Mussoorie.

At 57, the literary *eminence grise* of Mussoorie, is India's best-known writer of fiction, who has, amazingly, been able to eke a living almost exclusively out of writing since the age of 17. There were two brief stints of working odd jobs, but he adds, "Those were my struggling years. I was soon fed up and came to live in Mussoorie."

That was in 1964, and Ruskin Bond, author of some 200 short stories, a similar number of journalistic essays (including a monthly column for the US-based *Christian Science Monitor*), 40 children's books, four novels and, more recently, texts for coffee-table books, has not looked back since.

He hasn't needed to. Ruskin Bond's Mussoorie is the inspiration for his short stories and novels. It is, "the heart of India, an untapped source of vast human potential". For as Bond says, in his introduction to *Time Stops At Shamli* "India is really to be found in its small towns."

Ruskin Bond is to be found at Ivy Cottage, Mussoorie, which has become something of a tourist landmark. Being the literary don of a tourist resort has its pitfalls, as Bond has learned sometimes to his dismay. Everyone from local socialites to public school boys, who have grown up on a healthy diet of Ruskin Bond's fiction, wants to claim him.

Take a walk with him on the M… you are sure to be accosted by half-a-dozen people who want … just how their Mr Bond is today … ing the lobby of a hotel, Bond is … by an overwhelmed manager, "… Bond, we have been waiting for … for so long." Mr Bond smiles ge… always, exchanges a few polite … and carries on. Later over tea a… omelettes, … admits that … require co… ble skill to d… the adulati…

Bond's house in Mussoorie has become something of a tourist landmark. And the writer has discovered the pitfalls of being a local celebrity

MEETING RUSKIN BOND

SOUTH CHINA - MORNING POST (HONG KONG)

SUNDAY MORNING POST, MARCH 12, 1989

BOOKS

Bond bolsters a view of the gentler side of India

THE NIGHT TRAIN AT DEOLI AND OTHER STORIES by Ruskin Bond (Penguin, about $65)

SUE EARLE

GENTLE is not an adjective many people would think of applying to India. Ask the first-time visitor to the subcontinent what struck them...

his stories by addressing the "Gentle Reader". But as the character of these tales is revealed, so are the motives for his opening passage: "I use the old fashioned term to address you, because I like it and because I know that only the more gentle kind of person is likely to care much for my stories."

and friendships which he evokes in *Bus Stop, Pipalnagar*, one of the longer pieces in this collection. Like several of his stories, this is told by a young writer, scraping by on the few rupees he earns from selling stories and articles. His friends in the little town include the local barber, a rickshaw man, and an epileptic orphan, who makes a living as a pedlar in order to continue his studies.

Everyone hangs together and each helps the other. All of them want to leave Pipalnagar, and the narrator will be the first. When he is invited to Delhi for an interview with an important newspaper editor, his friends

children running naked through the rain: "Pipalnagar mud has a quality all its own; and it is not easily removed or forgotten. Only buffaloes love it because it is soft and squelchy. Two parts of it is thick sticky clay which seems to come alive at the slightest touch, clinging tenaciously to human flesh. Feet sink into it and have to be wrenched out. Fingers become webbed."

It's hardly surprising that everyone wants to get away from the place. Delhi, Calcutta, and Bombay are seething with people from small towns just like Pipalnagar, who have dreamt of making their fortunes if

surrounding houses and wondering if an aspiring author lurks behind them, tapping away on a rented typewriter. Nor shall I take a rickshaw without imagining that perhaps the driver has a friend who can produce a clean white shirt.

The story is typical of many a country town and its inhabitants and has a particularly well developed sense of people and place.

This quality exists to some degree in all the pieces in the collection. Although some of them are extremely short – just two or three pages – there is never any doubt as to where the reader is or who he is with. Particularly effective are the tales about chil...

awareness of the environment, especially the trees, which crop up so often in his stories. The elements often have a part to play, most spectacularly in *Sita And The River*, a story about a little girl whose home is washed away in a flood.

Weather is an important part of life in India, and its oppressive nature – the heat, the crisp winter mornings and chilly nights in the hills, and the heavy humidity before the monsoon rains come – is often conjured up in Bond's prose with a few well chosen words.

It would be easy to go on finding things to praise in this often thoughtful and perceptive book. But it would be wrong to lay bare all Bond's secrets

---

Bond

...le man

simple needs.

In an age when steamy sex and chiller thrillers are in vogue, we need a Ruskin Bond to bring us gently back to earth, to reawaken our senses to the natural beauty around us, especially the mountains that he loves and which have produced his most inspired work. ...tting at his desk in Ivy Cottage, a tumbledown, two-room cottage precariously perched on a spur in the hills of Mussoorie, Ruskin looks out from his picture window and sees and hears things we have become blind and deaf to. Like the man himself, his prose is simple and stark yet elegant and effective. Reading this collection of short stories, essays, poems and articles is literally like inhaling a lungful of fresh mountain air.

Much of his writing is in diary form, observations about people and places and things, not about palaces and kings. And here lies his true worth. His stories are about nothing unusual or kinky or extraordinary. He can write an entire piece on water, the sound of the rain on a tin roof, the bubbling of a brook, and make it sound like the greatest discovery made by mankind.

This is not the best of his work, nor is it the worst. But with Ruskin, there is

...IN THE ...NTAINS ...Penguin 251 ...Rs 250

Bond: an unconventional writer

no best or worst, just the steady output of a man in love with the written word, a man who lives, in his own words, in "a bulging, disoriented octopus of a hill station" which he loves as much, even though it does not create the atmosphere or background for money-spinning novels.

Now 60, Bond has no desire for that kind of notoriety either, perhaps never had. As he says: "Given the choice, I would not have done differently. When you have received love from people and the freedom that only mountains can give, then you have come very near to the borders of heaven." In the context of his self-imposed literary boundaries, he surely has.

The Gentle Voice of Indo-Anglian Literature

Ruskin Bond is the gentle voice of Indo-Anglian literature. He is the link between the British writers on India of the nineteenth century and the present-day Indo-Anglians. The nineteenth century writers may be divided into two broad categories: those who, like William Delafied Arnold and John Lang, wrote chiefly about the ... of the English in India; and writers like ... Hockley, Philip Meadows ... dyce who ...

CRITICAL ESSAYS

his childhood ayah, whose care makes her "My First Love;" "Untouchable" who consoles the author during a period of loneliness and fear; "The Kite-maker;" a tongawala; "The Bent-Double Beggar"; and "The Amorous Servant."

Bond perceives a pattern and a meaning in the humblest life. For instance, Kundan Singh, his servant, "was not very efficient, he ate more than most people, borrowed money, gambled in the bazar, drank raw country liquor, and generally overslept in the mornings." Bond dwells on his affairs with women, mostly married ones. Kundan ... defending the country. Yet the ... meaningful: "His youth had

---

Free Press Journal 19/4

NEW TITLES | 19 APRIL 1992

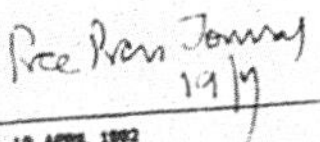

Ruskin Bond

...TREES STILL GROW IN DEHRA

Rolled Out from The Little Room

By Kavita Jaisingh

WHEN the desire to visit 'hills...alive with the sound of music', rings loudly in your mind but circumstances compel you to stay put, how do you resolve ...? Fortunately,

father's idea, that had survived much against his grandmother's wishes. Until one day, the latest addition was introduced — a python. The story actuates your interest as the python gets lost. Only to be found in a household predominated by women and an eccentric, visiting aunt who lets out an awful sob on learning of its presence. A hunt ensues but the python was absconding. And to quote Ruskin: "Aunt Mabel must have frightened it away." "Hush," said grandfather, "We ... aunt in

the best way of acquiring attention — by making oneself scarce. The less you have, the more you want, as the maxim goes.

"Wherever you go or whatever you do, MOST of your life will have to happen in your mind. And there is no escape from that little room," says Ruskin fighting up the sagacious side of his nature. It is admirable that a young Bond of 16 could write a story, in which, in spite of being ingrained in the idea that 'untouchables,' should be kept ...

person who ever left him ... thing, or an 'inherit... enough,' the art of writing ... puts it, Ruskin Bond ded... one of his best works to ... and his family'. Now ... they? Good 'ole Jeeves ... best short and sweet ... tion to our master ... only companion.

'I wandered lonely ... that floats high o'er ... hills,' said William W... that is very much ... an Wordsworth ... cloud gives ... everything, thus ... the vales and ... Bond too com... magnanimous ... breezes throu... downs.

... to want ... and una... the deo... d the tall ... above the ... rly morn... ds and the ... ntly proclaim ... r. The author ... ehradun and ... ees them their ... thanking them ... ve given him ... nces took away. ... could live in the ... serene woods, ... khuda, tonga

... time I saw Delhi, ... arallel between his ... ale's. It gets even ... ing when one learns ... of being profoundly ... his father, the only

Having ... ish Raj, the ... about ... tempts ... Indians ... Pigeons ... into a ... Benega... his ... British ... 'defe... boo...

Indian Express ... Page ...

Nation

A writer's life chronicled

DEHRA DUN – Exactly a year after being honoured with the Sahitya Akademi award, renowned English author Ruskin Bond has established another landmark in his literary journey by bringing out his autobiography, a poetic saga of his life and struggles.

Titled *Rain in the mountains* the work, just released, reflects greatly on the theme of nature in its various aspects.

Talking to UNI here, Ruskin Bond described it as "a book about a writer's life and nature."

"The seasons figure prominently in this autobiography and as do the mountains," the friendly man of the mountains said while talking animatedly about the book which is close to his heart, like a favourite child.

He went on to say, "One can see from this book why I have been staying up there in the mountains for the past 30 years."

Dehra Dun also comes into the book as it is basically my hometown and never away from my thoughts for long," said Bond who has recorded in many of his works his days as a small boy in the Doon of the 1940s. However, the autobiography mainly covers the period of Bond's life from the ... ties to the nineties, dealing with three decades in three ...

life, *Rain in the Mountains* ... across as a beautiful literary personal account of a lover of trees, flowers, birds and mountains.

"This is the most subjective ... works as it chronicles my str... over the years when I was no... earning much but somehow ... other I managed to eke out a living through my writing," said Bond who has become a legendary figure in Mussoorie where he has spent 30 long years of his life. "Bond Sahib's house" is a landmark in the popular hill-resort and is known to all locals.

"I selected my poems and essays for the autobiography keeping in mind the central theme of nature and its main facets," Ruskin Bond said while depicting nature in the book.

Also figuring in the work are descriptions of Prem, his adopted son, his children and grandchildren. Prem's son got married recently and even has a small son who nestled comfortably in the author's lap as he talked about his book, not to forget the family's pet dog, Tony.

The author is presently in Dehra Dun to get away from the severe winter at Mussorie.

Humorous accounts and descriptions of friends and acquaintances feature in Bond's autobiography. "I have refrained, however, from having a dig at those of my friends and acquaintances who are still living," he remarked jocularly.

Rain in the mountainside is not a chronological account of Bond's life and times. It is reflective and has remarkable depth. It moves backward and forward in time. Incidents of his school days at Bishop Cotton's in Shimla are recounted ...

'Wordsworth in prose'

The Lamp Is Lit: Leaves From a Journal

By Ruskin Bond

Penguin, Rs 250

to have lost sight, even, of his destination.

Words of Bond are words of nature, words of love. In him is kept the powerful sword of compassion, his own Excalibur, with which no one possessing a certain sensitivity can remain untouched. His stories are stories about a simple world, the world that exists amidst us but which we cannot touch or see. Therefore, some of us may choose to disbelieve him; we may say that all that he writes are untruths, his works ...

When I was ten, I was lonely...

Take It Or Leave It

Some Advice to Young Writers & Others

To avoid discussion or argument — wait until he (or she) is in the bathroom (or toilet), then deliver your ultimatum & be off before the other can get up or out.

Ruskin's advice to young writers and others.